KENNY COOKS AMERICA

'The greatest dishes are very simple dishes.'

Escoffier

'Nothing helps the scenery like ham and eggs.'

Mark Twain

'A man is in general better pleased when he has a good dinner upon the table, than when his wife speaks Greek.'

Samuel Johnson

KENNY COOKS AMERICA

Kenny Miller

PRION

First published in Great Britain in 1998 by PRION
32-34 Gordon House Road,
London NW5 1LP

A catalogue record of this book can be obtained
from the British Library

ISBN 1-85375-272-X

Cover and text artwork by Phillip Morrison

Text design by Kelly Flynn
Typeset by York House Typographic Ltd, London

Printed and bound in Singapore

ACKNOWLEDGEMENTS

To my extended family, who never stop telling me to both grow up and pack in the inebriated rubbish. Lovingly, however, they do tell me to keep on cooking.

To the late Bob Payton and the late Peter Cook. Both of whom influenced me greatly. With one I shared Diet Coke and chili dogs, with the other I devoured Margaritas and Crab Cakes.

To Diana, Princess of Wales. I was writing and worrying about fried chicken when I heard about her untimely death. (To me a somewhat humbling experience.)

To Ann Feachnie. She got me off the pots and into cooking.

To Andrew, my Editor, and his winsome assistant Catherine. Folk with misguided faith.

To Paul Durrant.

And finally to my 'main squeeze', Ms Allen, and our dog Henri Miller. Henri appreciates real food and real bones.

This book is dedicated to my late brother Clark — my best friend.

CONTENTS

INTRODUCTION 8

MY AMERICAN PANTRY 11

BEFORE LUNCH – BRUNCH 43

SOUPS AND STEWS 61

DRINKS, APPETIZERS AND SMALL
PLATES 81

BIG PLATES AND DINNER SALADS 97

SANDWICHES AND THEIR FRIENDS 155

SIDE ORDERS AND OTHER STUFF 185

JUST DESSERTS 195

THE LAST WORD 205

LAGNIAPPE 207

BIBLIOGRAPHY 211

INDEX 214

INTRODUCTION.

The United States of America is the grandmother of fusion cooking – a true melting pot and the spiritual home of culinary experimentation. Nowhere else on our planet can you experience such a rich blend of tastes and styles of cuisine.

The meeting of different cultures has had a profound effect from the very beginning. The rich cuisine forged by mixing the cooking of the first Spanish settlers with that of the native Mexican and American Indians is a great example. Through their vast global trading links the Spaniards' culinary efforts drew on their experiences in Africa, the Mediterranean and the Arab countries. While the native Indians in turn introduced the Spanish to corn, beans, chocolate, chiles and tomatoes. The outcome? Glorious food.

As history progressed many more cultures came to the Americas: eastern and western Europeans, Asians and Africans each bringing with them diverse cooking styles and new ingredients. The black slaves brought the seeds of okra from Africa, and these became a key ingredient of that Cajun institution, the gumbo. And where would the Rueben sandwich be without the bizarre German invention of sauerkraut? Or can you imagine Eggs Benedict without Samuel Bath Thomas's 'English Muffin'?

Travelling around America's food establishments provides an opportunity to sample some of the finest food to be tasted anywhere. You can try every ethnic cuisine from Jewish to Vietnamese, but what makes American cooking truly wonderful is that it just keeps on fusing to spectacular effect. Back in 1985 I remember eating in a Chino-Latino joint in lower Manhattan. Initially I laughed at the thought, but then, as the food arrived, I marvelled.

America is the place where people reinvent themselves and this goes for their food too. In addition to championing ethnic cooking and mixing it with other styles, Americans like to create new dishes. They do this with a pioneering passion, naming them like conquered peaks or frontier towns. They have given us everything from the the Caesar salad and Buffalo wings to eggs Benedict and the all-American hamburger. As with everything else in modern culture we owe a huge debt to the States. The history of 20th-century food is the history of American food.

To some this debt is a mixed blessing. Many European chefs have a derisive attitude toward American cooking. Rather than marvel at its diversity and innovation they only see the US as the overfed home of quantity and not quality. Even Americans share this view: John and Karen Hess wrote in their book *The Taste of America* back in 1977, 'How shall we tell our fellow Americans that our palates have been ravaged, that our food is awful, and that our most respected authorities on cookery are poseurs.' Continuing '...the dirty secret of American luxury dining is pre-cooked frozen food.'

America is the home of democratic, down-home, blue-collar cooking. But this is reason to celebrate, not hide in shame. They invented fast food and often have a no-frills attitude. But this is not the same as not caring. Many of the classic American dishes like the burger we often encounter in low-grade bastardized form. Should you ever meet the real thing (and if you read on and cook on you will), it is a rich and rewarding experience that has little in common with its fast-food phoney cousin. The lore, wisdom and care that go into American greats such as the barbecue, the hot sauce, the gumbo or the hamburger are as involved, exacting and esoteric as the most haute of European cuisines. Yet at the same time these dishes are happiest dressing down.

Real cooking is produced by folk who enjoy having fun, whilst making it happen. This is the one essential ingredient of my American cooking. All aboard.

Enjoy.

Kenny Miller

SERVINGS AND MEASUREMENTS

Most recipes for my dishes will serve 4–6 folk, according to appetites, unless otherwise stated.

I tend to use American cup measurements. Life's too short for all that weighing. It's a quick and easy method and an integral part of my style – one I hope you will adopt. There are metric and imperial measurements too but don't chop and change between them, you must follow one or the other.

Here's a list of British English names for ingredients used in this book for those of you unfamiliar with the American English.

BRITISH	AMERICAN
aubergine	eggplant
coriander	cilantro
cornflour	cornstarch
courgette	zucchini
double cream	heavy cream
pepper	capsicum
prawns	shrimp
rocket	arugula
spring onions	scallions
tomato purée	tomato paste

MY AMERICAN PANTRY

MY AMERICAN PANTRY

Why do we have a pantry? – to make quick suppers, sandwiches and five-star dinners really happen! There is no substitute for having a home-made pantry. It is the beginning to a truly happy kitchen life.

Pickled Chile Peppers

This is the most important jar in my pantry. Hopefully it will become the same in yours. Use it with every cold dish you make. Especially that midnight scallion, mayonnaise and soft-boiled duck egg sandwich.

12 small green jalapenos
1/3 cup olive oil (3 fl oz/75 ml)
2 white onions, sliced very thin
2 cloves garlic, crushed – not diced
3 cups cider vinegar (1 1/4 pints/700 ml)
2 cups white sugar (10 oz/250g)

1 tbl mustard seeds
1 tbl celery seeds
3 whole cloves
1 tsp black peppercorns
2 tsp onion salt
1 tsp turmeric

Stick the peppers in a 5-cup (2-pint/1 1/4 litre) jar.

Saute the onion and garlic in the oil over a medium heat, for about five minutes. Add all the other ingredients, except the jalapeños, and bring to a boil. Let cool. Pour the liquor over the jalapeños and immediately seal in a Mason Jar or something similar. Store in a dark place for three weeks or so, then enjoy.

My other favorite uses for jalapeños are in jelly, lollipops, jellybeans and ice cream. The ice cream is to die for. If I remember, by the time I reach the end of the book, I'll include a recipe. One just like you'll find at the Texan 'Great Jalapeño Lickoff' in San Angelo.

My favorite branded product for pickled jalapeños is the Mezzetta version out of Sonoma, California. 'Don't forget Mezzetta!'

As you'll soon gather chiles are pretty central to my way of cooking. Here is a brief lowdown on the varieties I use. Some are widely available, for others you'll need to search out speciality food stores:

Anaheim	A long green or red chile with a mild heat.
Cascabel	A small round red chile with a medium smoky heat.
Chipolte	Dried smoked jalapenos, they are dark brown, gnarled and medium hot.
Habanero	Also called the Scotch Bonnet (because of its shape), they come in all colours, have a burning heat and a tropical fruity taste.
Jalapeno	The classic green chile with a medium heat.
Poblano	A large red or green mild chile. When dried it is called Ancho and has a delicate smoky taste.
Serrano	Red or green, bullet shaped and hot, but with little flavor.
Thai	Small red and green and hot

Salsa

A salsa is an uncooked sauce. Never cook a salsa. Use a pestle and mortar to mix the ingredients. Simple.

Salsas originate from Mexico and, like the country, are colorful, moody, exciting and make your mouth want to dance. They are low in cholesterol, fat and calories and add a depth of flavor to any meal. Here is my favorite bunch of salsas.

A few personal rules for the successful execution of salsa:

Core tomatoes

Roast and peel all vegetables, including chiles and peppers

Use only fresh citric juices

Use only fresh herbs

No zany combinations — keep the flavors clean

Salsa Fresca

This is the salsa served up with tortilla chips in the ubiquitous Tex-Mex restaurants. It means 'fresh sauce'. Made the right way it is a wonderful salsa. The recipe makes about 2 cups.

3 green chiles (serranos if possible),
de-seeded and de-veined, then cut into fine
strips and diced
5 Roma tomatoes, roasted, peeled, then
cored and diced
1/2 cup (2 1/2 oz/60 g) red onion, finely diced
1/4 cup (1 1/4 oz/ 30 g) cilantro, coarsely
chopped

2 tbl dark Mexican beer
1 tbl olive oil
1/4 tsp garlic salt
1/2 tsp coarse-ground black pepper
1/2 tbl of lime or lemon juice
1/2 tbl snipped chives

Combine all ingredients and chill for no more than 4 hours.

Salsa Verde

Salsa Verde is a green salsa — not too difficult to work out, right? Its vital ingredient is the tomatillo. Tomatillos are berries from the physalis family and when removed from their husk they resemble unripe tomatoes and have a flavor similar to that of a gooseberry. If you can't find tomatillos for salsa verde, stick with its sister Salsa Fresca. Salsa Verde, like its sibling, is simply great with corn chips or as an addition to a sandwich.

Many restaurants serve a Chimichurri sauce as Salsa Verde. This parsley-based sauce is big in South American cooking, particularly Argentinian, but it's not my Salsa Verde.

2 cloves garlic, finely diced (sprinkle a little
salt on your chopping board – this way you
will be able to keep the oils from the garlic –
place the cloves on the salt and crush them
with the blade of your knife, then dice)
12 tomatillos, chopped
2 green jalapeños, de-seeded and de-veined

1 shallot, finely diced
4 scallions, finely chopped, including whites
1 tbl cilantro, coarsely chopped
1 tsp lime juice
1 tsp sugar
2 tsp sea salt
1 tsp coarse-ground black pepper

Combine all ingredients and chill before use.

Rattlesnake Salsa

The cascabel chile — a dried version of the little Italian cherry chile — is hot, with a nutty, fruity flavor. When shaken it rattles, hence the name (*serpiente de cascabel* is Spanish for rattlesnake). This salsa makes an excellent accompaniment to rich, meaty dishes. I first tasted this at Jimmy Schmidt's classic Rattlesnake Club in Detroit.

4 cascabel chiles, roasted and de-seeded
3 tbl cider vinegar
2 Roma tomatoes, roasted, cored and diced
1 small red bell pepper, cored, de-veined and finely diced

2 cloves garlic, crushed and diced
1 tsp fresh oregano
½ tsp allspice
pinch of garlic salt
1 tsp olive oil

Combine all ingredients in the mortar and blend real well. Chill.

Tropical Fruit Salsa

One of my favorite recipes. The first tropical salsa I made in the mid-1980s was a mango one. I thought no one else knew about it. Now it is everywhere. If you feel adventurous serve the salsa with home-made ice cream for dessert. A real winner.

4 jalapeño chiles, de-veined and de-seeded, finely chopped
1 cup (5 oz/125 g) mango, peeled, pitted and finely chopped – add the juice
½ cup (2 ½ oz/60 g) blood oranges, peeled, pithed and carefully chopped
½ cup (2 ½ oz/60 g) papaya, peeled, de-seeded and chopped

1 cup (5 oz/125 g) peach, blanched in sugar water, peeled and diced (after cooling of course)
2 tbl lime juice
2 tbl cilantro leaves, coarsely chopped
1 tbl olive oil
2 tsp fresh ginger, finely chopped
1 tsp brown sugar

Combine all ingredients at room temperature for 30 minutes and then mix with your pestle and mortar. Chill for 1 hour before serving. Enjoy, especially with chicken or fish.

Salsa Borracha

This salsa may sound complicated and the ingredients seem odd, but it is well worth the effort – both for the tastes and the colors. It is a key element in the *Barbacoa* – traditional weekend barbecue parties in areas like El Arroro in Mexico City, where the salsa is used as a relish on barbecued lamb. The cactus leaves are the paddles from the nopal cactus, also known as the prickly pear cactus. They taste like a cross between okra – they're also slimy – and green beans. They are available tinned. Having lost most of the 1980s drinking Margaritas, I now abstain from the potent agave juice. However, it is still an integral part of my cooking and helps to produce fabulous dishes. Use with grilled red meats.

4 ancho chiles, re-hydrated, de-seeded and diced

1 red onion, finely diced

2 cloves garlic, roasted and diced

6 Roma tomatoes, roasted, cored, de-seeded and diced

1 cup (5 oz/125 g) cactus, coarsely chopped

½ cup (4 fl oz/125 ml) Dos Equis or other dark Mexican beer

1 tbl silver tequila

½ tsp ground cumin

½ tsp paprika

½ tsp sea salt

½ tsp coarse-ground black pepper

Combine all ingredients and chill. Bring to room temperature before use.

Roast Corn Salsa

This is a vibrant salsa to make any dish or salad dance. As my buddy Lane says 'I love the smell of roast peppers in the morning', and this not simply because he is a fan of Robert Duvall, but because when you start roasting the chiles, corn and peppers, first thing, the intoxicating smell really makes you feel alive.

4 ears of corn

2 scallions, finely diced

2 anaheim chiles, de-seeded and diced

2 small red onions, finely diced

1 tbl fresh oregano, finely diced

2 small red bell peppers, de-veined, de-seeded and beautifully diced (by this I mean you take your sharp knife through the inner

skin of the pepper, to leave a juicy, colorful pepper flesh)

2 cloves garlic, diced

1 chipotle en adobe, diced

1 tbl lime juice

½ tbl cider vinegar

½ tsp sea salt

To roast the corn: shuck the outer husk and place the cobs over a bare flame, blacken as much as you can without burning, then cut the kernels from the cobs.

Mix with all the remaining ingredients and keep at room temperature. Cold corn sucks. Serve with chicken or as a side order – but not with corn chips.

When choosing corn follow these simple guidlines:

Choose: husks that are tightly closed
golden and clean silks
stems that look freshly cut

Pierce a kernel and reject the cob if juice fails to spurt out.

(Also reject the store, if they fail to let you do this.)

Use corn as soon as possible after purchase.

Pico de Gallo

This is a very common salsa in Mexico, often served as an optional accompaniment at the table. It is made with just these four raw ingredients – chiles, tomato, onion and cilantro. The name derives from the way it is eaten with the thumb and forefinger, resembling the pecking of a rooster.

6 jalapeños, de-seeded and finely diced
10 Roma tomatoes, roasted, cored and diced
1 large white onion, finely diced

⅓ cup (2 oz/45 g) cilantro leaves, coarsely chopped

Mix all ingredients and cool slightly before use.

Xnipec Salsa

Xnipec is Mayan for 'dog's breath'. But really the salsa is named for the way it makes your nose run! It's a salsa like an R 'n' B band jamming – flowing until your nose runs. Try it with scrambled eggs and you'll never look back, I promise. At the Pinch-a-Pollo Restaurant in Austin, Texas, they serve it with an achiote-marinated grilled chicken breast. Achiote is a paste made from the softened seeds of the annato tree, mixed with garlic and vinegar.

1 red onion, finely diced
juice of 5 limes
1 peach, peeled, pitted and chopped
2 habañero chiles, de-seeded and finely diced

2 tomatoes, cored and chopped
1 tbl cilantro leaves, coarsley chopped
1/2 tsp sea salt
1/2 tsp coarse-ground black pepper

Soak the onion in the lime juice for 30 minutes. Add the other ingredients and chill. Yields 2 cups (16 fl oz/500 ml). And remember, if your fingers haven't already told you, this salsa is extremely hot.

Seasonings

I suggest you keep a bunch of your own home-made seasoning mixes in your pantry. It takes only a few to make sure your comfort foods or fancy dinner parties are for real. Store-bought or the mail-order nonsense just do not compare. Seal your mixes tightly and store away from direct sunlight. Direct light, heat and moisture will impair their quality. A cool, dry cupboard is best.

Use the seasonings as soon as you can and make sure you label them. I guess I don't need to tell you to buy only good quality herbs and spices. Always taste before mixing, and use within three months. Many of these mixes are key ingredients in the recipes that follow.

Kenny's Seafood Seasoning

There are many uses for this seasoning from dusting scallops, shrimp and oysters before cooking to garnishing seafood dishes just before they hit the table. However you use it, I promise you will not be disappointed. Having said that, some of my experiments with seafood seasoning have made me cry — but I guess that's what cooking is all about.

1 tbl kosher salt
1 tbl celery seed
1 tbl black peppercorns
1 tbl mustard seeds
4 bay leaves, crushed
1 tsp ground cloves

1 tsp ground ginger
½ tsp mace flakes
½ cinnamon stick, crushed
1 tbl cayenne pepper
1 tbl cardamon seeds

Combine all ingredients and store with an airtight lid.

Kenny's French Quarter Seasoning

I originally invented this seasoning mix for French Fries, but it is now a regular 'garnish' in it own right in my kitchens. I love to dust plates with it and also use it to impart an extra dimension to some of my dishes. For maximum flavor use Hungarian paprika, it beats the pants off Spanish every time. Maybe source it from Paprika Weiss on Second Avenue, between 80th and 81st streets in Manhattan.

2 tbl paprika
2 tbl cayenne pepper (must be freshly ground)

2 tbl garlic salt
1 tbl garlic powder
1 tbl celery salt

Mix all ingredients well and store in an airtight container. Always mix in a large bowl, otherwise you'll end up making a mess – trust me. Before you begin to cook, transfer the seasoning to a 'shaker' – most stores carry them now. Shakers are perfect for accommodating even seasoning and quick dusting.

Garlic salt is also readily available, but why not try making your own – it's a gas and will lead you into a whole new world of pantryonomy (my newest word). Call me if you get stuck.

My Blackening Seasoning

A wonderful mix of herbs and spices for coating meat or fish before 'blackening' – searing in a white-hot skillet. It is a method of cooking popularized by the Cajun chef Paul Prudhomme.

5 tbl paprika
4 tbl thyme
2 tbl oregano
4 tbl cayenne
2 tbl coarse-ground black pepper

2 tbl garlic salt
1 tbl garlic powder
1 tbl celery salt
1 tbl crushed celery seeds
1 tbl onion powder

Mix thoroughly and store in an airtight container.

My Saute Seasoning

Any fast cooking needs help to ensure the dish doesn't become one-dimensional.

1 tbl garlic salt   *1 tbl ground white pepper*
1 tbl garlic powder   *1 tbl coarse-ground black pepper*
1/2 tbl onion salt   *1/2 tbl crushed mustard seeds*

Mix thoroughly and store in an airtight container.

My General Seasoning

This is a seasoning base I like to use for 'big' dishes.

1 tsp black peppercorns   *2 tsp paprika*
1 tsp celery seeds   *1 tbl mustard powder*
1 tsp cayenne   *1/2 tsp garlic salt*
1/2 tsp dried thyme   *1 tbl brown sugar*
1/2 tsp marjoram   *1 tsp ground cumin*
1/2 tsp oregano

Combine all ingredients in your mortar, crushing with the pestle until most of the peppercorns are broken up. Seal tightly.

Curry Seasoning

When I make this seasoning myself I like to pretend I'm a real 'masalchi'. But I guess I'll never know if I'm good enough. This version is something of a short-cut method. Use your imagination to work out how to roast and grind the original products for the best results.

6 tbl dried red chile flakes
1 tbl coriander seeds
2 tsp cumin seeds
1 tsp mustard seeds
1 tsp coarse-ground black pepper
2 tbl dried curry leaves, crushed

½ tsp ginger
1 tbl turmeric
½ tsp ground cinnamon
2 cardamom pods
1 pinch ground cloves

Place all ingredients on a baking tray. Roast in the oven on a medium temperature for 20 minutes. Let cool then pound the hell out of the mix in your pestle and mortar or in a blender. Store in an airtight container and keep in a dark cupboard.

Pepper Seasoning

3 tbl coarse-ground black pepper
1 tbl ground white pepper
2 tbl cayenne pepper

½ tbl finely ground black pepper
½ tbl celery salt
1 tsp ground mustard seeds

Combine all ingredients and store in a jar.

My Chili Seasoning

2 tbl cayenne

1 tbl paprika

1 tsp oregano

1 tsp ground cumin

1 tsp garlic salt

1 tsp onion powder

Combine all ingredients and store in a jar.

Hot Sauces

The musical instrument known as the accordion was for the Nazis the 'devil's bellows', whilst Mark Twain called it the 'Steinway of the stomach' Obviously it's not to everyone's taste. It's the same with hot sauces, you either love them or loathe them. Yet, I feel, if you can begin to love them your passions will start to run deeper.

The main culprit of the 'dangerous' hot sauces is the habañero chile. It is by far the hottest edible item on this planet, so be careful. Hot sauces have achieved something of a cult status in the States. There is a cottage industry out there of lovingly crafted hot sauces, some better than others but always with great names – Screaming Sphincter, Pain is Good, Scorned Woman, Capital Punishment, Blair's After-death Sauce, Vampfire, Hellfire and Damnation, Jump Up and Kiss Me. But, as ever, the fun of home-made is best. Or are you just too lazy?

Kenny's Hot Hot Sauce

This recipe makes about 2 cups (16 fl oz/500 ml). Store in an airtight container.

1 habañero chile pepper
2 carrots
1 medium white onion

1 cup (8 fl oz/250 ml) distilled white vinegar
2 cloves garlic
juice of 1 lime

Puree ingredients in blender. Pour into a non-metallic saucepan and slowly bring to boil. Allow to simmer for a few minutes then cool – properly. Strain very well and pour into a sterilized container. Leave in the dark for two weeks before use. I warn you – this is good, fruity and hot.

Kenny's Hot Sauce

2 jalapeños, de-seeded and finely diced
1 tomato, peeled, cored and de-seeded
1 medium red onion, finely chopped
2 cloves garlic, peeled
1/2 papaya, peeled, de-seeded and diced

2/3 cup (5 fl oz/150 ml) cider vinegar
1 tsp fresh lime juice
1/2 tsp sea salt
pinch of ground cinnamon

Puree the vegetables. Scald the vinegar with the remaining ingredients then take off the heat and mix with the puree. Let cool then pour into a sterilized bottle. Seal tightly.

Ketchups

There is no shame in having a brand-name bottle of ketchup in your pantry. But there is blame to be apportioned if you have never tried to make your own. It is a wonderful way to impress your guests and satisfy yourself. Home-made ketchups make great condiments and can be used to pep up stock or stew.

Ket-tsiap (Chinese for 'picked fish') is a vinegar-based sauce. Everyone has heard of tomato ketchup, but what most people don't realize is that this is just one type amid a potentially limitless list. Why not try making it with wild mushrooms, papaya, mango, plantains or elephant garlic instead? Anything goes.

Georgeanne Brennan, a cook from Yolo County, California, makes a tangy-sweet Yellow Tomato Ketchup using all the sweet spices — ginger, coriander, cloves and cinnamon. It's great with grilled pork chops. Here's my more traditional sauce.

10 tomatoes, skinned, cored and chopped
1 medium red onion
1 medium red bell pepper
1 tbl olive oil
1/2 cup (2 1/2 oz/60 g) raisins

1/4 cup (2 1/2 oz/60 g) brown sugar
1 orange, peeled and diced finely
2 tbl red wine vinegar
1 tbl soy sauce
1 tsp Worcestershire sauce

Saute the tomato, onion and bell pepper for five minutes in the oil over a high heat. Remove from the heat and encourage the tomatoes to break. Add the rest of the ingredients, cool properly and refrigerate. Check flavor after 1 hour.

Mustards

Of all the items in our pantry mustard must be one of the oldest. All the ancient civilizations record its use. I'm quite sure however, none of them ever produced anything as insipid as the product known as 'American' mustard. It is made from white mustard seed and is blended with sugar and wine. It is pale yellow, thinner, milder and sweeter than other mustard. In France – the world's biggest importer of mustard seeds – it cannot be legally marketed as mustard. Fortunately, with the advent of 'modern American' cooking, there are now endless variations on this basic and uninspiring product. They make great condiments, and accompaniments to meat and fish and just about anything else.

One of my favorites is a Chile Rojo Twister mustard made by Mark Miller of Coyote Cafe fame. Below is my own chile mustard and also some other favorites.

Chile Mustard

1 tbl mustard seeds
1 tbl cilantro leaves, coarsely chopped
1 tsp water
1 tsp olive oil
3 tbl Dijon mustard
2 tbl mayonnaise
½ tsp cayenne

1 small red jalapeño, de-seeded, de-veined and finely diced
1 tsp tomato puree
2 scallion stalks, finely chopped, including whites
juice of 1 fresh lime
½ tsp garlic salt

Crush the mustard seeds in a pestle and mortar with the cilantro, water and oil. Mix all the other ingredients, then add the mustard mix. Transfer to a Mason jar or similar container and seal.

Onion Mustard

2 scallion stalks, finely chopped
1 small red onion, finely chopped
1 clove garlic, minced
5 chives, snipped – this means you chop the
chives very carefully and slowly (I have a
saying for a chef who chops slovenly –
I cannot repeat it here, but it is very fitting)
5 tbl Dijon mustard

1 tbl dry mustard powder, mixed to a smooth
paste with water.
1 tbl sour cream
1 tbl olive oil
1/2 tbl creamed horseradish
1 tsp onion salt
1 tsp coarse-ground black pepper

Combine all ingredients. Transfer to a Mason jar and seal. Leave for 24 hours before use.

Lime Mustard

5 tbl Dijon mustard
1 tbl mayonnaise

zest of 3 limes
1 tbl lemon juice

Combine all ingredients and chill.

Garlic Mustard

5 cloves garlic, minced
5 chives, snipped
4 tbl Dijon mustard

1 tbl sour cream
1 tsp cayenne pepper
1 tsp garlic salt

Combine all ingredients and chill.

My Mayonnaise

Life is too short to spend it counting calories, measuring grams of fat and trying to decipher encoded secrets on food labels. As a consequence I strongly suggest you make your own mayonnaise — raw eggs and all. There is a definitive mayo recipe on page 150. This is my simple recipe which I use when mixing in flavors. My favorite additions are garlic, chipotle en adobe, anchovies, cilantro and roast tomato. Please yourself.

3 large egg yolks
4 tbl lemon juice
½ tsp sea salt

1 ½ cups (12 fl oz/325 ml) good olive oil
1 tsp snipped chives

Have all ingredients at room temperature before starting. I strongly advise you not to use a food processor, unless you don't want a silky, smooth and light sauce. Whisk the egg yolks with half the lemon juice and the salt until smooth. Keep on whisking as you drizzle in the oil. At the end add the rest of the lemon juice and the chives.

Chutney

I wish this condiment had a different name. Ever since I was a kid, the omnipresent jar of store-bought pickle used to stare at me from the lunch table. I hated the sweet noxious mess, and it knew. The name always summons this terrible vision, yet when properly prepared these relishes make wonderful accompaniments to a whole host of dishes.

Chutneys can be hot, mild, sweet or sour. I like them hot and chunky, although some folk prefer to blend them and have them smooth. The key to chutneys is to push the flavor of the fruits, so keep cooking times down to a minimum.

The name is of Indian origin. They were first commercially produced in the United States in the late 1800s by a Mr Henry Heinz. Sound familiar?

Peach-Habañero Chutney

5 peaches, boiled in water until the skin begins to peel off; rinse under cold water, peel and remove the stone and dice the flesh
1 habañero, de-seeded and finely diced
1 white onion, finely diced
1/2 tbl fresh ginger, grated
1 tbl peanut oil
1/2 cup (2 1/2 oz/60 g) brown sugar

1 tbl lemon juice
1/2 cup (4 fl oz/125 ml) white vinegar
1 tbl raisins
1 tbl yellow mustard
1/2 tsp cinnamon
1/4 tsp allspice
1/3 cup (2 oz/45 g) mint leaves, finely chopped

Over a moderate heat saute the habañero, onion and ginger for five minutes in the peanut oil. Add the peach flesh, sugar and lemon juice, and cook for a further 5 minutes. Remove from the heat and add the vinegar. Stir in well, making sure the edges of the pan are scraped clean. Replace on the heat and reduce until the ingredients have thickened – about 5 minutes. Stir in the remaining ingredients and allow to cool.

Store in an airtight jar.

Mango, Papaya and Green Chile Chutney

*2 mangoes, peeled, pitted and cut into
¼ inch cubes; retain the juices and add
them in with the mango cubes
1 papaya, halved, de-seeded and the meat
scooped out; gently chop the meat and again
retain the juices.
1 small red onion, finely diced
½ tbl fresh ginger, grated
2 tbl peanut oil*

*½ cup (2 ½ oz/60 g) brown sugar
3 green jalapeños, de-seeded, de-veined and
finely diced
½ cup (4 fl oz/125 ml) cider vinegar
1 small yellow bell pepper, cored and finely
diced
½ tsp ground cinnamon
½ tsp ground cloves
pinch of cumin ground*

Saute the onion and ginger for 3 minutes in the peanut oil. Add the mango and papaya flesh and juice, sugar and jalapeños. Cook for a further 3 minutes. Remove from the heat and add the vinegar, yellow bell pepper and spices. Mix in well then return to the heat. Cook until thick – about 3 minutes, then let cool. Beware of letting it become mushy.

Refrigerate in a Mason jar or similar container.

Vinaigrettes

Texan rocker Joe Ely keeps his fingernails long so they click when he plays the piano, and is gonna keep them that way until the swallows get back from Louisiana. I keep a store of vinaigrettes and, just like Joe Ely, I'm gonna keep my pantry that way until the swallows get back from Texakarna.

House Vinaigrette

I use this dressing on everything salady. It's excellent. My other favorite vinaigrettes are – blueberry, raspberry, hazelnut, herb and mustard. Use my House recipe and add your favorite ingredients.

3 tbl olive oil
1 tbl red wine vinegar, never white
1 clove garlic, crushed

½ small red onion, minced
pinch garlic salt
pinch coarse-ground black pepper

Blend all ingredients for 3 minutes. Store in a dark cupboard for one week before use and remember never to run out, otherwise I ain't coming over.

Oils

Flavoured oils are buckets of fun. All the top chefs are playing with them now. Jean-Georges Vongerichten of Vong and Jo-Jo's in Manhattan and London does a great Shrimp Salad with Curry Oil. Charlie Trotter in Chicago presents a Seafood Sausage with Baby Greens, Pineapple, Sage and Red Chile and Ginger Oils. Back in Manhattan, Larry Forgione of An American Place fame, serves up Roast Cod with Cranberry Beans and Rosemary Oil. And Mark Miller, owner of The Red Sage in Washington DC and the Coyote Cafe in Sante Fe, uses canola oil to make an Apple-Cinnamon Oil, with which he dresses a Prairie Field Salad to accompany Native Goat Cheese Fritters. Get the idea? The options are endless. Play with them.

Chive-Jalapeño Oil

This is my personal favorite (surprised, huh?). Along with adding great flavor this oil just looks so cool and real pretty drizzled around a centred salad.

3 red jalapeños, de-seeded, de-veined and finely diced
2 green jalapeños, de-seeded, de-veined and finely diced
1 red onion, finely diced
1 bunch snipped chives
1 medium carrot, cleaned and very finely diced
1 small yellow bell pepper, roasted, peeled,

cored and finely diced (let it cool before dicing)
1 tsp garlic salt
1 tsp coarse-ground black pepper
1 1/2 tsp poppy seeds
1/2 tsp mustard seeds
2 1/2 cups (1pt/600 ml) olive oil
1 tbl cider vinegar

Combine all the vegetables and dry ingredients then mix in the oil and vinegar. Pour into a tightly sealed container. Store in the dark for 3 days. Shake well before use.

Marinades

Rubs and marinades are used to add layers of expression and character to our basic foods. Both are simple to produce and use. Sometimes, particularly with real fresh produce, like a freshly caught trout, they are not necessary. But with cheap cuts of meat, which are potentially the most flavoursome, a zesty marinade is vital to help produce an excellent, tender meal.

Rubs are, of course, meant to be dry marinades; not all mine are.

Tequila and Cilantro Marinade

¼ cup (1 1/4 oz/30 g) sugar
2 cups (16 fl oz/450 ml) cider vinegar
2 red jalapeños, de-seeded, de-veined and
finely diced
2 tbl gold tequila

2 tbl cilantro leaves, coarsely chopped
½ cup (4 fl oz/125 ml) lime juice
2 tbl olive oil
1 tbl dried oregano
1 tbl mustard seeds

Mix all ingredients and store in the dark for 24 hours before use.

This marinade is best for white chicken meat or seafood.

Tomato and Bourbon Marinade

8 Roma tomatoes, roasted, peeled, cored and
diced
½ cup (4 fl oz/125 ml) Jack Daniels
1 small red onion, finely diced
3 shallots, finely diced
3 cloves garlic, finely diced
½ cup (2 ½ oz/60 g) snipped chives
½cup (2 ½ oz/60 g) brown sugar

1 cup (8 fl oz/250 ml) cider vinegar
1 tbl soy sauce
1 tbl oyster sauce
1 tsp cayenne pepper
1 tsp celery salt
1 tsp coarse-ground black pepper
2 tbl lime juice

Combine all ingredients and seal tightly. Store in a dark cupboard for at least 2 days.

Use with red meats.

Barbecue Marinade

Use this and you will never buy a store-bought barbecue product again – or maybe just Curley's famous, all-natural, hickory barbecue sauce, from Kansas.

As Bobby Seale, co-founder of the Black Panthers and true barbecue pit master, says, 'Barbecuing is a truly American act of soulful hospitality', which 'can change a grumpy attitude to a pleasant kind of sereness'.

2 red onions, finely chopped
4 garlic cloves, minced
⅓ cup (3 fl oz/75 ml) Worcestershire sauce
2 cups (16 fl oz/500 ml) ketchup
1 tsp liquid smoke – this is widely available
(it is the condensation from inside the smoke house)

½ cup (4 fl oz/125 ml) tomato puree
1 tbl molasses
1 tbl raisins
1 tsp tamarind pulp – available from East Indian stores
⅓ cup (3 fl oz/75 ml) red wine vinegar
1 cup (8 fl oz/250 ml) chicken stock

Place all ingredients, except the stock, in your food mixer and blend for 2 minutes. Meanwhile heat the stock over a moderate temperature. Add the blender mix and cook for a further 3 minutes or until the mix is syrupy.

Transfer to an airtight container. Feel free to use with all your favorite barbecue recipes.

Red and Black Pepper Rub

A great rub for dry barbecuing all kinds of meat and fish.

1 tbl ground cumin

1 tbl coarse-ground black pepper

2 tbl cayenne

3 tbl paprika

1 tbl oregano

1 tbl thyme

½ tbl crushed celery seeds

½ tbl mustard seeds

1 tsp garlic salt

½ cup (2 ½ oz/60g) brown sugar

Mix all ingredients and store in an airtight container.

Ancho-Olive Oil Rub

6 ancho chiles, re-hydrated, de-seeded and
chopped

1 tbl olive oil

1 tsp brown sugar

2 garlic cloves, finely diced

1 tsp garlic salt

1 tbl orange juice

2 tsp cayenne

1 tbl paprika

½ tsp celery salt

1 tsp dried oregano

Combine all ingredients, mix well and keep at room temperature.

The key is to make this rub sticky, but not runny. It is perfect for meats. In particular it works wonders on a leg of lamb. Forget the old adage of rosemary with lamb – smother the puppy in some serious flavoring.

Salad Dressings

Salad dressings should be packed with flavor. Otherwise you'll need to use too much dressing and end up drowning the salad stuffs, especially in the spring and early summer when they are at their most tender.

Kenny's Ranch Dressing

3 cloves garlic, finely diced
2 cups (16 fl oz/500 ml) buttermilk – for you
'healthy living' nutters
1 tbl lime juice
1 heaped tbl sour cream
1 cup (5 oz/125 g) avocado flesh, mashed
1 small red bell pepper, cored, de-veined and

finely diced
1 tsp cayenne
2 tbl snipped chives
1 tbl cilantro leaves, coarsely chopped
1 tbl olive oil
1 tbl rice wine vinegar

In a mixing bowl combine all ingredients and whisk well. Chill until you are nearly ready to use. Allow to reach room temperature, whisk again and then use.

Remoulade Sauce

This is a New Orleans classic, stolen from France and adulterated. A basic remoulade is a mayonnaise sauce flavored with mustard, tomato sauce, anchovy essence, gherkins, capers, parsley and chervil. Of course in Louisiana it gets the funky treatment.

There are many versions and a multitude of books to choose a recipe from. The right one is simply the one you like best – it's as basic as that. The sauce is usually served with boiled shrimp or chilled crabmeat. I prefer it in a broiled shrimp sandwich, but I think you will find infinite uses for remoulade, unless, that is, you sport a toque instead of a tattoo.

1 tbl lemon juice

1 tbl olive oil

3 scallions, including whites, finely chopped

1 rib celery, finely diced

2 red jalapeños, de-seeded, de-veined and finely diced

2 cloves garlic, finely diced

2 cups (16 fl oz/500 ml) mayonnaise

1 tbl capers, coarsely chopped

1 tbl creamed horseradish

2 tbl wholegrain mustard

½ cup (4 fl oz/125 ml) ketchup

1 tbl parsley, finely chopped

1 tsp garlic salt

1 tsp coarse-ground black pepper

½ tsp celery salt

Combine all ingredients and chill.

Honey-Mustard Dressing

One of my all-time favorites.

2 cups (10 oz/250 g) coarse-grain mustard

1 tbl honey

1 tbl olive oil

1 tbl cider vinegar

½ tbl lime juice

½ cup (4 fl oz/125 ml) orange juice

1 tsp garlic salt

1 tsp cayenne pepper

½ tsp coarse-ground black pepper

Combine all ingredients and chill for 6 hours.

Kenny's Soy Sauce

I love to use Kikkomans soy sauce to enliven soups, stocks and stews, but sometimes I feel its intricate flavors can be lost if used in big dishes and if you just add more of the sauce the dish becomes too salty. Save it for fast sauces and sauteed dishes. My adapted soy sauce is easier to use.

1 tbl peanut oil

1 white onion, finely diced

1 green jalapeño, de-seeded, de-veined and finely diced

1 clove garlic, finely diced

1 tsp coarse-ground black pepper

3 anchovy fillets, minced

1 tbl Balsamic vinegar

1 tsp paprika

1 tsp oregano

1/2 tsp sea salt

1/2 tsp thyme

1 cup (8 fl oz/250 ml) Kikkomans soy sauce

Heat the oil and saute the onion, jalapeño and garlic for 10 minutes. Add the rest of the ingredients, except the soy sauce, and simmer for 5 minutes. Take off the heat and add the soy sauce. Strain and allow to cool. The sauce is now ready to 'wake up' your dishes.

Tomato French Dressing

This French dressing has the heart of a *diable* and will help set the soul of your salad on fire.

2 tbl mixed fresh, chopped herbs

1 tbl white sugar

1 tbl cider vinegar

2 tsp lemon juice

1 cup (8 fl oz/250 ml) olive oil

1 red jalapeño, de-seeded, de-veined and finely diced

1 tsp sea salt

1 tsp coarse-ground black pepper

3 chives, snipped

1 small red onion, diced

8 tomatoes, roasted, peeled, cored and diced

1 tsp celery salt

Combine all ingredients in a mixing bowl and whisk. Store in an airtight container and place in a dark cupboard for 2 days. Whisk again before use.

My Blue Cheese-Thousand Island Dressing

2 cups (16 fl oz/500 ml) mayonnaise
1 cup (8 fl oz/250 ml) sweet chile sauce
1 each small red and yellow bell pepper,
cored and diced extremely fine
1 tbl sweet pickle relish
2 chives, snipped

1 onion, grated
2 hard-boiled eggs, grated
½ cup (2 ½ oz/60 g) crumbled Roquefort
1 tbl sour cream
1 tsp garlic salt
1 tsp coarse-ground black pepper

Combine all ingredients and mix well. Leave at room temperature for 30 minutes and then use or refrigerate. If you refrigerate the dressing, make sure you cover it tightly and bring it to room temperature before use.

Butters

Flavored butters are a great contribution to anyone's cooking. As with everything else in my pantry they simply and inexpensively elevate your cooking to new heights. Flavors I enjoy adding to butter include garlic, roasted peppers, cilantro, mustard, chipotles and rosemary.

Garlic Butter

Garlic changes its flavors according to the time of year it is harvested. In summer it's usually sweet and in winter very strong.

The word is from the old English 'garleac' which means 'spear leak', although I prefer the American Lunch Counter slang where the bulb has been referred to, over the years as Bronx Vanilla, Halitosis and Italian Perfume.

If you feel the need to make garlic bread this is the butter for you. May I suggest you use some of it in the actual bread recipe, along with melting it over the grilling bread.

1 ½ cups (8 oz/185 g) unsalted butter, softened
2 cloves garlic, finely diced
2 chives, snipped

½ tsp garlic salt
½ tsp celery seeds
1 tsp olive oil

Gently mix the ingredients together, then transfer to your serving dishes and refrigerate.

BEFORE LUNCH
- BRUNCH

BEFORE LUNCH – BRUNCH

Brunch and the big breakfast are an American institution. For many Americans breakfast is the most important meal of the day. Many restaurants, like the Cat's Incredible Cafe on Soquel Drive in Aptos, California, open early and serve a huge variety of tantalizing breakfast foods all day long.

At the Cat's you can start with three extra-large eggs, home fries, and choice of toast, English muffin, home-made muffin or biscuit with ham, country or link sausage – all for six bucks! Or maybe you'd prefer two extra-large eggs, home fries and biscuits with country gravy for five bucks; and who could resist strawberry almond waffle topped with whipped cream?

For those of you who don't have a breakfast diner nearby, these recipes are perfect for turning the Sunday morning after the night before into a lazy day of feelgood gastronomic indulgence.

In terms of equipment for brunch, a mandolin is a prerequisite to make sure you don't lose too many flavors to the chopping board, and in particular for creating a perfect hash brown. A home sausage-maker can be helpful and will seriously impress your friends. Most American diner breakfasts are cooked on a large iron grill plate called a 'flat top'. You can achieve similar results on a large iron skillet.

Waffles

Nowadays we can readily purchase waffles from any food store, take them home and just pop them in the toaster or under the grill. But where's the fun in that? Many folk just don't have a waffle iron – a web-patterned sandwich toasting affair into which the batter is poured. But those who do can treat their friends and family to a most uplifting start to the day.

The versatile waffle can be served with just about anything. In Baltimore they traditionally serve kidney stew with their waffles on Sundays. Despite my anarchic attitude to cooking and eating I prefer a fresh fruit garnish and maple syrup, although adding savory ingredients can actually be fun and allows you to make a different type of lunch item. Just add your additional ingredients on top of the batter when it's in the iron. The following recipe should make eight waffles.

2 cups (10 oz/250 g) all-purpose flour	*3 eggs, beaten well*
1 tbl baking powder	*1/3 cup (2 oz/45 g) butter, melted*
pinch of salt	*1/2 tsp vanilla extract*
2 tbl brown sugar	*maple syrup and fresh fruit to garnish*
1 1/2 cups (12 fl oz/375 ml) milk	*icing (confectioners') sugar, for dusting*

Warm up your waffle iron, greasing both the top and the bottom irons. Mix together the flour, baking powder and salt. Sift into the sugar in a large bowl and mix well. Whisk together the milk, eggs, butter and vanilla. Pour the liquid into the flour and gently combine. Do not mix for too long – a few lumps are welcome. Pour into the centre of your iron and spread towards the edges. Close your iron and cook for about 2 minutes. Cut the waffles on the diagonal and serve with plenty of maple syrup poured over them, fresh fruit on the side and icing sugar shaken over the whole lot.

The Western

The Western is an omelette sandwich. The omelette is made with green bell peppers, chopped ham and onions, and is served on or in white bread or toast. It originated in the deepest Mid-West where folk work hard and, as a result, need hearty breakfasts.

5 large eggs, separated
pinch of garlic salt
2 stalks snipped chives
1/2 tsp coarse-ground black pepper
1 1/5 cups (6 oz/150 g) smoked ham, diced
seriously fine
1 small red onion, diced very fine

1 small green bell pepper, roasted, topped
and tailed, membrane removed, julienned
and diced real small
2 tbl butter
4 slices of thick white bread, buttered on the
outside and grilled

Beat the egg whites in one bowl and the yolks in another. Add the rest of the ingredients to the yolks except the whites and bread. Mix well. Keep at room temperature. Turn on your grill – the overhead one – to a medium heat. Melt the butter in a skillet and season with salt and pepper. Add the whites to the yolk mix and beat again. Pour into the skillet and cook until the edges will lift. Place under the grill and watch it puff up. After about 4 minutes it will be nearly ready. Take from the heat and leave to settle for 2 minutes – have another slurp on your Bloody Mary, we can't cook brunch without a Bloody. Slip the omelette on to your chopping board and cut into quarters. Place two quarters on a slice of bread, points touching, top with another slice of bread and cut diagonally across the sandwich. Repeat with the other half. Garnish with fresh fruit and get ready to become full.

Bagels

A bagel is, of course, a yeast bun with a hole in the middle. It originated with the Ashkenazi Jews who introduced Yiddish culture to the US. The bagel was first mentioned in print around 1892, in Israel Zangwill's novel *Children of the Ghetto*... "Moses treated his children to some beuglich, or circular twisted rolls". Without a doubt the best bagels in America are found in New York. This recipe should make between 14 and 16 bagels. Before baking you may want to get funky and sprinkle with poppy seeds, sesame seeds or onion pieces or whatever. It's up to you, as usual.

1 pack dried yeast
1 cup (8 fl oz/250 ml) warm milk
1 tsp sugar
3 ½ cups (18 ½ oz/510 g) all-purpose flour

½ tsp salt
1 egg, separated
4 tbl butter, at room temperature

Mix the yeast with the milk and sugar. Allow them to get together for 20 minutes. Sift the flour and salt into a mixing bowl. Whisk the egg white until frothy. Add the yeast mix, softened butter and egg white to the flour mix. Combine together and make a soft dough. Knead on a floured surface for 5 minutes until the dough becomes elastic. Return to the bowl, cover with oiled cling film and leave in a warm spot for 90 minutes.

The dough should double in size. Punch the dough back, then divide into 16 pieces. Roll each piece out and form them into circles – you can work this out. Arrange the rings on a greased baking sheet. Cover with a dry cloth and allow to double in size. Pre-heat the oven to 400°F/200°C/gas mark 6. Bring a large pan of water to the boil, then take down to a simmer. Drop each bagel in the water for 20 seconds. Drain the bagels, then place back on the greased baking tray. Beat the egg yolk with 1 tbl water and brush over each bagel. Bake for 20 minutes or until you like the glaze on the surface. Eat straight away.

Pancakes

A flat top griddle is a flat piece of heavy iron used primarily for cooking pancakes in restaurant (although I tend to use mine more for blackening these days). If you don't have one, which is more than likely, using your largest iron skillet – preferably a non-stick one – should work fine.

Pancakes are certainly one item that usually taste better at home. My favorite place to eat them out is Polly's Pancake Parlour at Sugar Hill, New Hampshire – a 50-year-old joint, initially opened to promote their maple syrup but now a revered pancake parlour which overlooks the luscious fields of Polly's farm. Although according to those who know, Vermont is *the* maple syrup state.

2 cups (10 oz/250 g) all-purpose flour
2 tbl sugar
4 tsps baking powder
½ tsp salt

1 ⅓ cups (11 fl oz/325 ml) milk
1 egg, beaten
2 tbl unsalted butter, melted
maple syrup and fresh fruit to garnish

Combine the flour, sugar, baking powder and salt in a large mixing bowl. Thoroughly mix together the milk and egg. Gently mix in the dry ingredients and then the butter. Lightly grease your griddle or your thickest and widest skillet. For each pancake pour ¼ cup (2 ½ fl oz /60 ml) of batter on to the skillet. Cook until the top of the pancake begins to bubble, then flip over and cook for a further 2 minutes. Remove to a warm plate and keep warm. Serve three pancakes, stacked on top of each other, with butter, maple syrup and a garnish of fresh fruit.

Eggs and Wet Belly Hash

Hash just means a mixture of chopped ingredients. Wet Belly Hash – or Cornbeef Willie as it is known elsewhere – is a mix of potatoes, onions and corned beef topped with eggs, and is said to be the original dish. The best I've ever eaten was at Phillips Restaurant, College Corner Pike, in Oxford, Ohio. It cost five bucks, although with a side order of biscuits and gravy, toast and jelly, the bill went up a little. They served the hash with fried apples. Corned beef is usually brisket that has been cured in salt. The name comes from where the beef was cured – in the corn barn, or so I'm told. But I bet you can find a different story.

3 cups (1 lb/450 g) corned beef, finely chopped
3 cups (1 lb /450 g) potatoes, coarsely chopped
3/4 cup (6 fl oz/175 ml) whipped cream
1/3 cup (2 oz/45 g) onions, finely chopped
3 tbl parsley, finely chopped

1/2 tsp garlic salt
1/2 tsp coarse-ground black pepper
2 tbl butter
8 eggs
2 cups (16 fl oz/500 ml) Salsa Fresca (see p. 15)

Mix together the corned beef, potatoes, cream, onion, parsley and seasonings. Pre-heat the oven to 375°F/190°C/gas mark 5. Melt the butter in a skillet then add the corned beef mix. Cook for about 15 minutes – nearly burn it. You'll need to keep stirring and scraping. Make 8 little pits in the hash and crack an egg into each indentation. Place the skillet in the oven for about 10 minutes, or until the eggs are cooked your way. Be careful, the handle will be hot.

With a spatula ease out two eggs, with hash, for each portion. Obviously add on any hash that falls off. Centre on a plate and surround with Salsa Fresca. I like to garnish with snipped chives. And if my guests are of the hungry type – smother it in Hollandaise (see p. 52).

Grits with Ham, Red-eye Gravy, Eggs and Biscuits

'True grits,
more grits
Fish, grits and collards.
Life is good where grits are swallered.'

Roy Blount Jr, *One Fell Soup*

This little combination of recipes is a classic southern country breakfast. Grits are finely ground dried, hulled corn kernels which can be prepared in a variety of different ways. The name is from the old English *grytt* for bran. They're not to everyone's taste, but I just love 'em.

I have chosen to use quick-cooking grits – for the obvious reason – but you may feel you want to be authentic and cook the real thing. Good luck if you do. They require attention if you want a creamy result – maybe use a double boiler.

1 cup (4 ½ oz/125 g) quick-cooking grits
1 ½ cups (7 ½ oz/185 g) grated Cheddar cheese
1 tsp garlic, minced

8 tbl unsalted butter
½ cup (2 ½ oz/60 g) scallions, chopped
2 eggs, beaten
¾ cup (6 fl oz/175 ml) milk

It's easy for me to say to cook the grits according to the package instructions – but I will, because it makes sense. Stir in the cheese, garlic, butter and scallions. Pour into a greased casserole dish and allow to cool. Pre-heat the oven to 375°F/190°C/gas mark 5. Mix in the eggs and milk and place in the oven. Bake for one hour.

Meanwhile bake your biscuits (see below), grill your ham, make your gravy and poach your eggs. The key to poaching eggs is to add white wine vinegar to your boiling water – I know you'll use fresh and hopefully free-range eggs.

Southern style country ham is an uncured pig's hind which is cooked into a salty, delicious, rich meat. I could euologize for pages on southern hams, but I won't bore you, other than to say preparing hams can reach levels of high art. If you cannot order a ham from Billy Higdon's in Lebanon, Kentucky, speak to your butcher about securing a good ham and be sure to roast with tons of cloves and some brown sugar and maybe a dash or two of bourbon.

To make your red-eye gravy, add black coffee to the debris and juices in your ham roasting pan and mix well over a low heat. You should see a reddish eye form in the middle of the gravy. This is liquid fat and is mighty fine tasting.

Biscuits

White Lily is the classic flour used to make biscuits. This Knoxville, Tennessee company goes back 100 years. It is the flour of the south and the product's colour matches its name. You can do just fine though with sifted all-purpose flour.

This is a recipe I love to use from the nationally renowned New York Times writer Craig Claiborne. Along with James Beard and M.F.K. Fisher, he is a god-parent of all things good about American cooking.

3 cups (1 lb/450 g) sifted flour
3/4 tsp salt
1/2 tsp baking soda

4 tsp baking powder
2/3 cup (4 oz/100 g) lard
1 1/3 cups (11 fl oz/325 ml) buttermilk

Pre-heat the oven to 425°F/220°C/gas mark 7. Sift together the dry ingredients into a mixing bowl. With your fingers 'cut' in the lard until the mix resembles cornmeal. Gently mix in the buttermilk to a smooth blend. Transfer to a floured surface and work the dough until you feel it is well mixed. Roll the dough out until is evenly 2.5cm (1/2 in) thick. With a cookie cutter cut out 5cm (2 in) biscuits. Keep dipping the cutter in flour to stop you making deranged shapes and work quickly. Remember to punch the biscuits out and not twist.

Place the biscuits on a floured baking tray and bake for 12–15 minutes or until the tops are brown. You want to finish them just as everything else is finishing. You will be busy but she'll appreciate it. Just make sure she has a Bloody ready for you or at least a new Hawaiian shirt.

Eggs Benedict

I've being cooking this dish for many years and this is my very own definitive version. The whole dish relies on your own ability to poach eggs and to produce a gloriously rich and spicy Hollandaise sauce. This makes a perfect breakfast for two. I like to serve mine with skinny fries but this is just a suggestion.

For the Hollandaise sauce
4 egg yolks, beaten
1 egg, beaten
1 tbl double cream
1 tsp cider vinegar
pinch of cayenne
pinch of garlic salt
2 tbl unsalted butter, melted

4 eggs, poached
2 English muffins, halved
2 slices ham
fruit to garnish
Salsa Fresca, prepared in advance (see p. 15)
1 tbl chives
Kenny's French Quarter Seasoning (see p. 22)

Over a double boiler gently heat together all the Hollandaise ingredients except the butter. After 5 minutes slowly drizzle in the melting butter. Over your double boiler keep whisking until the sauce is nearly thick. Unless you want to serve immediately you want to keep it relatively loose, otherwise the sauce will begin to solidify. To stop this, keep the sauce covered and warm. If you add color and flavor, by dropping in snipped chives or finely chopped jalapeños, keep whisking your sauce because they can drag down and separate the sauce.

Whilst your Hollandaise is settling and your eggs are poaching do all the following: butter your English muffins and grill them over a low heat. Grill your ham. Ideally the ham should be Canadian Bacon but you can use your favorite ham, just make sure it is good quality. Cut it to cover the muffin, then grill it. Anything can be used as a fruit garnish – I like to use blueberries, blackberries and redcurrants.

To assemble it all, on a pretty plate place the salsa at 12 o'clock. Arrange the fruit at 6 o'clock. Situate the muffin halves side by side in the middle of the plate. Top each muffin slice with a ham slice. Top each ham slice with a poached egg. In turn top the eggs with skinny fries (if you've made them), then smother with the Hollandaise. I like to garnish with snipped chives and my French Quarter Seasoning but I'll leave it up to you – just enjoy.

Blueberry Muffins

Muffins take no time at all to cook. They also smell and taste great. Give them a go and you may surprise yourself. Any fruit or base cereal works well, so feel free to experiment.

2 tbl butter, softened
2 tbl shortening
1/3 cup (2 oz/45 g) sugar
1 egg
3/4 cup (6 fl oz/175 ml) milk

1 3/4 cups (8 3/4 oz/215 g) all-purpose flour
1 tbl baking powder
1/2 tsp salt
2/3 cup (4 oz/100 g) frozen blueberries –
slightly drained

In a large mixing bowl cream the butter and shortening. Slowly add the sugar, beating until the mix is light and fluffy. Add the egg and beat well. Then add the milk to the batter and gently fold in. Sift the flour, baking powder and salt together and mix into the batter, but do not mix too hard – lumps are good. Mix in the blues.

Lightly grease your muffin tins. Spoon in batter ²/₃ up the cup. Bake at 375°F/190°C/gas mark 5 for 25 minutes, or until a toothpick comes out clean. Remove from the pan immediately and serve. I always like to eat them with a Scarlet O'Hara cocktail – peaches, sugar, bourbon, lime juice and ice, but you may simply prefer maple syrup and a fresh fruit garnish.

Green Chile Cornbread

Cornbread was being eaten thousands of years before wheat arrived in North America, although in those really early days – the Mesoamerican civilizations – corn was a grass with tiny cobs. Cornbread is another fast and easy dish to make, just like muffins.

1 cup (5 oz/125 g) all-purpose flour
1 ¹/₂ cups (7 ¹/₂ oz/185 g) coarse cornmeal
1 tbl baking powder
2 tsp sea salt
3 tbl sugar
2 cups (16 fl oz/500 ml) full-fat milk

3 eggs, beaten
3 jalapeños, de-seeded, de-veined and finely diced
2 tbl chives, finely snipped

Mix all dry ingredients. Mix all wet ingredients. Combine. Heat the oven to 375°F/190°C/gas mark 5. Butter a pre-heated small loaf tin or your cast-iron cornbread skillet and pour in the batter. Place in the oven for 20–25 minutes if you're using a 23cm (9 in) pan, less for skillets. Let cool slightly before turning out and serve immediately with chive butter.

My Own White Loaf

'There is nothing more positive than bread.'

Fyodor Dostoyevsky

You just have to cook your own bread at least once. If you don't, you deserve to eat fish scales. In my opinion there is nothing more satisfying than your own white loaf. I suggest you don't let anyone know you're baking. Keep it to yourself and have a private grilled cheese and jalapeño sandwich, whilst the bread is still warm of course. I've said it before, but this truly is ambrosia.

2 packs of dried yeast
5 tsp granulated sugar
3 cups (1 1/4 pints/700 ml) lukewarm water
10 1/2 cups (3 lb 4 1/2 oz/1.3 kg) 'bread' flour

4 tsp salt
1/4 cup (1 1/4 oz/30 g) lard

Stir the dried yeast and a tsp of the sugar into the water. Leave for 15 minutes or until a frothy head kicks off. Meanwhile, mix the flour, salt and remaining sugar in a large mixing bowl. Rub in the lard. Add the yeast mix. Knead to a soft dough.

Now the first stage of hard work. Spread a clean area with a thin layer of flour. Transfer the dough to the surface and knead for 10 minutes, until the dough is smooth, elastic and no longer sticky. Keep sretching the dough with the heel of your hand. Clean the mixing bowl and replace the dough. Cover with lightly oiled cling film and keep in a warm place. The dough should rise after about 1 1/2 hours. Return to the floured surface and beat the hell out of it – what you're actually doing is knocking the air out. This should take 5 minutes. Divide into 3 equal pieces. Shape into loaves – keep your hands dusted in flour whilst you work.

Grease your 8 1/2 x 4 1/4 x 2 3/4 inch loaf pans and drop in the dough. If you haven't got the right size loaf pan I'm sure you can work it out. Again you need to cover with oiled cling film and leave to prove – let it rise to double its size. For a crispy crust – brush the risen dough with salted water, then sprinkle over with flour before baking. Pre-heat the oven to

450°F/230°C/gas mark 8. Bake the loaves for 30-40 minutes. You know the loaf is ready when it sounds hollow. To ensure the whole loaf is crusty, remove from the pan and bake for a further 5 minutes. I prefer it soft – I cannot ever wait to eat my home-made bread.

The fun thing with this base bread is the numerous shapes, textures, flavors and toppings you can incorporate: a shiny finish can be achieved by glazing the dough with a beaten egg and a pinch of salt. After glazing, you could sprinkle it with poppy seeds. You may even wish to roll the dough into a cottage loaf, a bloomer, rolls or a baguette – anything really, if you have the correct tins. Whatever you choose, have fun.

Huevos Rancheros

Rancheros means 'ranch style' – you cook them any way you wish. Huevos Rancheros is gloriously executed by Chef Stephen Pyles, owner of the Star Canyon in Dallas. He often serves it with avocado-tomatillo salsa. My version may appear to be complicated – it is – but it just needs a little forward-planning. The results are definitely worth the effort.

2 poached eggs per serving

Ranchero saute mix
1 medium white onion, diced
1 stalk celery, diced
1 small red bell pepper, de-seeded and diced
4 cloves garlic, finely diced
2 tbl peanut oil

Ranchero stock mix
2 jalapenos, de-seeded, de-veined and finely diced
1 small green bell pepper, de-seeded and diced
4 tomatoes, cored and diced
4 cups (1 3/4 pints/1 litre) chicken stock
1/2 tsp ground cumin
1/2 tsp ground coriander
1 tsp coarse-ground black pepper
1 tsp thyme
1 tsp oregano
1 tbl fresh lime juice
2 tbl hot sauce (not Tabasco)

For the re-fried beans
5 cups (2 pints/1 1/4 litres) chicken stock – store-bought is fine
2 cups (10 oz/250 g) black beans or pinto beans, soaked overnight
4 cloves garlic, minced
2 red onions, minced
2 red jalapenos, de-seeded, de-veined and diced
1 anaheim chile, de-seeded, de-veined and diced
5 tbl olive oil
1 tsp ground cumin
1 tsp garlic powder
1 tsp oregano
1 tsp thyme
3 stalks scallions

To garnish
cheese, grated
Salsa Fresca, (see p. 15)
sour cream
cilantro leaves

Saute the vegetables in the oil until the celery is soft. Keep warm. Then boil all the stock ingredients for 10 minutes. Allow to cool a little bit and add the sauteed vegetables. Take back to the boil then remove from the heat and keep warm.

To cook the beans: take the stock to the boil, add the beans and cook for 20 minutes. Saute the vegetables, except the scallions, in 3 tbsp of the oil until the onion is soft. Add the softened vegetables and the seasoning to the beans. Cook for 10 minutes – keep stirring. Remove from the heat and keep warm.

Heat the remaining olive oil and saute the scallions for 3 minutes. Add the beans and cook for 5 minutes. You will need to stir and scrape continously.
Poach your eggs making sure they are syrupy. Grate the cheese of your choice – I

generally use a mix of Monterey Jack, sharp Cheddar and Red Leicester. Top with Salsa Fresca and sour cream and garnish with cilantro leaves. If you wish, just before you serve the dish, dust with French Quarter Seasoning (see p. 22).

Green Chile Sauce

This wonderfully versatile sauce can be used in place of the ranchero sauce. It's a steal from Cafe Pasquals in Santa Fe, New Mexico, where chef Katherine Kagel has been an inspiration to many cooks over the years. Ideally we need 1 lb of anaheims. They are hard to find, so I suggest you use 1 ¹/₂ cups (8 oz/185 g) green jalapeños and 1 ¹/₂ cups (8 oz/185 g) green bell peppers prepared the same way.

1 ¹/₄ cups (6 oz/150 g) white onion, chopped
your way, it don't matter too much
1 clove garlic, finely diced
2 tbl peanut oil
3 cups (1 lb/450 g) anaheim chiles, roasted,
de-veined, de-seeded and finely diced

1 cup (8 fl oz/125 ml) chicken stock
¹/₂ tsp garlic salt
¹/₂ tsp coarse-ground black pepper

Saute the onion and garlic in the peanut oil until the onion is soft. Add the rest of the ingredients and cook over a medium heat for 10 minutes. Allow to cool, then puree in your blender for a couple of minutes, until smooth.

Hash Browns with Rumbled Eggs

In the early 1900s the great Mississippi riverboats became floating palaces. Palaces which served awesome breakfasts. Unfortunately the only Mississippi riverboats I've been on served warm Lite beer and steamed hot dogs.

This is an old-fashioned breakfast. Rumbled Eggs are nothing more than scrambled eggs made with a little whipping cream. The key to making good Hash Browns is too mix the ingredients extremely well before a slow cooking.

4 large potatoes, boiled, peeled, grated and
left to cool
1 small onion, finely diced
1 tsp celery salt

1 tsp My General Seasoning (see p. 23)
1/4 tsp coarse-ground black pepper
3 tbl unsalted butter

Gently mix the potatoes with the onion and the seasonings. Heat the butter in a 30cm (12 in) skillet (if you know what bacon drippings are and have some, drop some in the skillet too). Keep the heat moderate. Evenly spread the potato mixture over the skillet. Press the potato down. Scrape from the edges to stop overcooking. Cook for 10 minutes. Without worrying about your hash falling apart, gently flip over and cook for a further 5 minutes. Spread evenly over four plates and top with your rumbled eggs. Simple and highly enjoyable.

Ham and Eggs Alexandria

This old version of ham and eggs was on my first ever brunch menu.

1 1/3 cups (8 oz/180 g) mushrooms, sliced
1 12 oz/300 g can artichokes, chopped
1/4 cup (1 1/4 oz/30 g) unsalted butter
1 1/2 tbl all-purpose flour
1 cup (8 fl oz/250 ml) milk
1/2 cup (2 1/2 oz/60 g) Gruyere cheese

2 tsp My General Seasoning (see p. 23)
3 English muffins, halved and toasted
6 slices of baked ham
1 hard-boiled egg, sliced
1 hard boiled egg, grated
pimento-stuffed olives, chopped

Saute the mushrooms and artichokes in a little of the butter for a few minutes. Make a white roux out of the rest of the butter and the flour. Gradually add the milk until thick. Add the cheese until it's melted. Stir in the mushroom mix and add the seasoning. Set aside and keep warm.

Place the muffin halves on plates. Top with a slice of ham. Spoon the sauce over each muffin. Garnish with a slice of egg, grated egg and olives. Try to serve warm.

At Hinky Dinks in Oakland, California – the famous Pacific-themed bar of 'Trader' Vic Bergeron, inventor of such classic cocktails as The Suffering Bastard and Dr Funk of Tahiti – they served ham and eggs, Hawaiian style. This was with canned pineapple and banana. Not quite as big a hit with me as some of his famous cocktails.

SOUPS AND STEWS

SOUPS and STEWS

Probably nothing else in the cook's repertoire is as important to the happiness of a family dinner table as their soups or stews. (Although I do think home-made bread comes a close second, in warming the ties that bind.) Stock is the vital ingredient. May I suggest you buy a comprehensive French cookery book on stocks to make sure you produce a consistently true product. One by Madeleine Kamman would do the job.

Gulf Coast Gumbo

No one can cook a gumbo better than me. Unfortunately everyone who cooks gumbo believes this about themselves. A gumbo is a one-pot stew thickened with okra. Beyond this it is hard to define, but suffice to say you will always desire a second bowl. A favorite dish of the early slaves, the name comes from 'ngombo', the Bantu name for okra.

I had my first and worst gumbo at Dookey Chase's in New Orleans, a soulfood restaurant immortalized by Ray Charles. However, I went on a learning curve and came to see gumbo as one of the most satisfying meals to cook and eat.

1 cup (8 fl oz/250 ml) peanut oil
2 cups (10 oz/250 g) all-purpose flour
4 cups (1 ¼ lb/500 g) white onion, sort of
finely chopped
1 cup (5 oz/125 g) green bell pepper,
chopped
1 tbl garlic salt
½ cup (2 ½ oz/60 g) parsley, finely chopped
1 cup (5 oz/125 g) celery, chopped
½ cup (2 ½ oz/60 g) scallions, chopped
10 cups (4 pints/2.4 litres) fish stock
1 tbl garlic, minced
1 ½ cups (12 fl oz/375 ml) white wine

1 tbl Worcestershire sauce
3 tbl Kenny's Seafood Seasoning (see p. 21)
2 tbl Louisiana Hot Sauce
1 cup (5 oz/125 g) okra, chopped
3 cups (1 lb/450 g) crawfish or uncooked,
peeled shrimp
1 ½ cups (8 oz/185 g) picked crab meat
3 cups (1 lb/450 g) strong-textured fish,
cubed (a white fish like drum, snapper,
grouper or hake would be good)
2 oysters per dish – shucked of course
cooked white rice – hot, of course

Make a dark roux with the oil and the flour. Add to this the onions, bells, garlic salt, parsley, celery and scallions. Stir frantically for 20 minutes. Keep adding a little stock until you have a thick paste.

Stir in the garlic, wine, Worcestershire, ⅓ of the seasoning and hot sauce. Heat up.

In a large bowl bring the rest of stock to the boil. Add the roux mix and okra. Stir for 5 minutes. Turn the heat down and simmer for 2 hours.

Add all the seafood, except the oysters, and cook for a further 45 minutes on a low heat.

Remove from the stove and add the rest of the seasoning. Let settle for 10 minutes and serve.

Place 2 oysters in each bowl and spoon over your gumbo. Centre each bowl with cooked rice.

Always serve your gumbo with cornbread.

Crackling Cornbread

Crackling is the most wonderful by-product of a roast pork loin. However, it does take some careful consideration. Cut the skin off your roast. Dice into bite-size pieces and place fat down on a baking tray. Pre-heat your oven to 225F°/110°C/gas mark 1/4. Place the tray in the oven for 4 hours, until the fat is rendered and the skin crispy. Remove the cracklings with a slotted spoon and drain. Dispose of the fat properly, once it has cooled down.

The next bit is up to you – either sprinkle with salt and eat, mix into salads or use in cornbread.

1/3 cup (2 oz/45 g) sifted all-purpose flour
1 1/2 cups (7 1/2 oz/185 g) cornmeal
1 tsp baking powder
1/2 tsp salt
2 eggs, beaten
2 cups (16 fl oz/500 ml) buttermilk

1/2 cup (4 fl oz/125 ml) milk
1/2 cup (2 1/2 oz/60 g) crackling, diced small
1 tbl red jalapeno, de-seeded, de-veined and finely diced
1 1/2 tbl butter

Pre-heat the oven 350°F/180°C/gas mark 4.

This recipe is for a 9 x 2 inch black skillet. But use whatever you like to bake in. These days you can find skillets of all shapes and sizes. Even chile and cactus shaped skillets exist. Obviously this will mean varying the cooking times.

Sift the dry ingredients together. Mix in the eggs, buttermilk and milk. Add the cracklings and jalapeños.

Heat the butter in the skillet. When it is hot pour in the batter and bake for 25 minutes, or until a toothpick comes out clean.

Serve immediately.

Fierce Crab Soup

This soup is from Maryland. It resembles a gumbo but somehow manages to allow the crab to still hold fiery centre stage. The inspiration for this dish is St Mary's County between Chesapeake Bay and the Potomac, where, amid the plantation homes, tobacco fields and river coves, you'll find a plethora of taverns selling all things crabby.

1 large onion, finely chopped
2 ribs celery, diced
1 green bell pepper, cored and finely chopped
peanut oil
2 tbl unsalted butter
5 cups (2 pints/1 ¼ litres) fish stock
1 cup (5 oz/125 g) rice
1 cup (5 oz/125 g) okra, diced

1 tbl Kenny's Seafood Seasoning (see p. 21)
½ diced tomato
1 tsp Worcestershire sauce
1 tsp hot sauce
1 cup (5 oz/125 g) sweet potatoes, cubed and parboiled
3 cups (1 lb/450 g) crabmeat, mixed dark and white
brown sugar and snipped chives to garnish

Saute the onion, celery and bell pepper in a little oil until the onion is soft. Bring the stock to boil. Add the rice, okra, seafood seasoning, tomato and Worcestershire. Cook for a further 10 minutes. Lower to a simmer and add the hot sauce and potatoes. Keep stirring until the rice is nearly cooked. Add the crab and the butter, then cover. Leave for 15 minutes.

Portion into bowls and garnish with sweet potato confetti – sweet potato cut very thin and deep fried. And sprinkle over brown sugar and chives.

Cioppino

What gumbo is to the south and chowder is to the north-east, cioppino is to San Francisco – an institution in its own right. It was originally a Liguarian fish stew brought over by Italian immigrants. As with other regional signature dishes, every cook thinks he has the best recipe. It should be made with six kinds of fish and six kinds of shellfish and, some folk say, calamari. The shrimp, of course, should not be peeled, and cooking them in what I call old pasta water is vital for authenticity. This is quite simply the water you boiled your Saturday pasta in.

Rose Pistola on Columbus Avenue, North Beach is the place to try it. Chef Hearon is a God and my inspiration for this recipe. I strongly recommend his *La Parilla* cookbook.

2 large onions, diced
1 tbl parsley, finely chopped
2 cloves garlic, minced
4 cups (1 1/4 lb/600 g) tomatoes, diced
1/2 cup (4 fl oz/125 ml) olive oil
2 cups (16 fl oz/500 ml) dry white wine
1/2 cup (4 fl oz/125 ml) tomato puree

2 bay leaves
1 tsp oregano
1 tbl Kenny's Seafood Seasoning (see p. 21)
1 cup (8 fl oz/250 ml) fish stock, or clamato juice
6 cups (2 lb/900 g) mixed seafood – see below

Saute the onions, parsley, garlic, and tomatoes in the oil until the onion is soft. Add 1 cup (8 fl oz/250 ml) wine and bring to a simmer. Mix in the puree, bay leaves, oregano and seasoning. Cook for 10 minutes. Add the rest of the wine and the stock. As soon as bubbles begin to appear add the seafood.

Which seafood you use is up to you. Just remember not to overcook it. Also, keep the delicate ingredients back until the firmer ones are nearly ready.

Pepperpot Stew

Slaves, back in the 1700s, were already cultivating many of the crops of their African homelands. Plants like yams, gungo peas, shaddocks, ackee and callaloo. Callaloo is a leafy vegetable like spinach or kale. It's indigenous to the Caribbean and its main contribution to world cooking is its role in the Pepperpot Stew.

3 cups (1 lb/450 g) callaloo, or fresh spinach
1 10oz/250 g ham hock
12 okra, sliced
½ cup (2 ½ oz/60 g) parsley, finley chopped
1 rib celery, finely chopped
4 scallions, including green parts, chopped

½ tsp thyme
1 red jalapeno, de-seeded, de-veined and finely diced
2 tbl Pepper Seasoning (see p. 24)
water
1 ½ cups (8 oz/185 g) crabmeat

If you are using callaloo, rather than spinach clean the leaves and blanch them for 3 minutes.

In a large pot cover the ham hock with water. Boil for 30 minutes. Add the okra, parsley, celery, scallions, thyme and jalapeño. Bring back to the boil, add the seasoning and then simmer for 2 hours. As soon as the ham is fork tender, remove and peel off the skin. 'Pull' the meat and return to the pot. Add the spinach and crab. Turn off the heat and let sit for 10 minutes.

Portion the soup equally between 6 soup bowls and serve.

Carolina Perlow

Perlow is cuisine of the water. It comes from the so-called Low Country around Charleston and the state coastal plain from Pawleys Island southward to the Savannah River. It is a kissing cousin of the pilau – the rice and meat dish that appears in so many cultures around the world. For folks around Charleston perlow is their dish and a real 'oo-la-la'. I like to serve a green salad and cornbread with my perlow. But I guess it's up to you.

1 large onion, chopped
1 tbl peanut oil
4 ½ cups (1 ½ lb/675 g) plum tomatoes, roasted, peeled, seeded and chopped
½ tsp red pepper flakes or crushed red peppers
3 tbl parsley, finely chopped
1 tsp garlic salt
2 cups (10 oz/250 g) long grain rice

3 cups (1 ¼ pints/700 ml) shrimp stock – it needs to be rich (a strong fish stock will be a good substitute)
4 ½ cups (1 ½ lb/675 g) shrimp meat – peeled and uncooked
snipped chives
4 slices bacon, diced and fried until crispy and crumbled

Saute the onion in the oil over a low heat until soft. Add the tomatoes, red pepper flakes and parsley, cook for a further 5 minutes. Add the garlic salt, rice and stock and bring to a simmer. Cover and cook for 20 minutes. Fluff up the rice and add the shrimp. Take off the heat and cover. Leave for 10 minutes.

Portion between 4 plates and garnish with snipped chives and the crumbled bacon. I suggest keeping the plates in the oven for 10 minutes before serving. Also give a little stir before presenting to your guests.

New England Clam Chowder

This is the true chowder. The name comes from *chaudiere* – French for a three-legged, heavy iron pot.

Authentically the ratio of the basic ingredients should be 2:2:1 – two parts clams, two parts potato and one part onion. But it doesn't matter too much, just as long as you don't overcook the soup.

Ideally the clam used should be a quahog, the hard-shelled 'venus mercenaria'. Its powerful abductor muscles keep it firmly shut under refrigeration and so flavor and texture are retained.

1 cup (5 oz/125 g) white onion, diced
1 clove garlic, finely diced
2 oz/45 g slab bacon, diced and grilled until crispy
1 tbl butter
2 cups (16 fl oz/500 ml) clamato juice or fish stock
2 cups (10 oz/250 g) potatoes, peeled and diced to 1/2 inch

1 tbl Kenny's Seafood Seasoning (see p. 21)
3 cups (1 lb/450 g) shucked clams
3 3/4 cups (1 1/2 pints/875 ml) milk
2 1/2 cups (1 pint/625 ml) double cream
1 tsp sea salt
1/4 tsp thyme
1/4 tsp cayenne
1/4 tsp coarse-ground black pepper

If you have not prepped up the ingredients beforehand, your chowder will take a long time to cook. Do it my way and you have a fast chowder. One you can start yesterday.

Saute the onion, garlic and bacon in the butter for 3 minutes. Transfer to a larger pot and add the clamato juice. Bring to a simmer and add the potatoes and the Seafood Seasoning. Cook for 10 minutes. Add the rest of the ingredients, mix in well, then take off the boil. Cover and let sit for 10 minutes. Stir again. Return to the heat and simmer for 10 minutes. Serve immediately. (Dusting with paprika makes a nice garnish.)

Despite being bit of a tourist trap and a huge apparel operation, the Black Dog Tavern on Martha's Vineyard, Massachusetts cooks up a great chowder. It also has the best bakery on the island and a breakfast to die for. And you can experience something close to nirvana if you manage to secure a seat overlooking the fishing piers.

Long Island Clam Chowder

This is actually more of a Brooklyn Chowder. A steal from the ancient Lundy Bros restaurant on Emmons Avenue where the chowders are excellent. Not to mention their 3-inch buttermilk biscuits.

1 ¹/₂ cups (8 oz/185 g) salt pork
2 medium potatoes, peeled and diced to
¹/₂ inch
1 white onion, coarsely chopped
2 ribs celery, finely diced
1 small green bell pepper, cored and finely diced
4 medium carrots, diced
water

³/₄ cup (6 fl oz/175 ml) clamato juice
4 plum tomatoes, skinned and diced
1 tbl Kenny's Seafood Seasoning (see p. 21)
2 bay leaves
1 tsp thyme
1 tsp sea salt
1 tsp coarse-ground black pepper
1 tbl tomato puree
12 large clams, steamed and shucked

In your biggest pot layer the salt pork, potatoes, onion, celery, bell pepper and carrots. Top with water and bring to the boil. Lower to a simmer and add the clamato juice, tomatoes and half of the seasonings. Cook for 20 minutes. Add the remainder of the seasonings and tomato puree. Stir in well and cook for 30 minutes. Top with more water if your chowder begins to stick. Take off the heat and add the clams. Cover and leave for 10 minutes. Return to the heat and simmer for 15 minutes. Serve immediately with buttermilk biscuits or plain crusty bread.

Tortilla Soup

This chicken-flavored soup is unbeatable. It's one of the signature dishes of Dean Fearing, chef at the Mansion on Turtle Creek in Dallas. This is my version.

corn oil
5 6-inch flour tortillas, coarsely chopped
4 cloves garlic, finely diced
2 tbl cilantro leaves, finely chopped
1 onion, finely chopped
1 cup (8 fl oz/250 ml) tomato puree
1 tsp ground cumin
1 tsp Curry Seasoning (see p. 24)

2 bay leaves
7 1/2 cups (3 pints/1.8 litres) chicken stock
1 tsp sea salt
1/2 tsp cayenne
1 chicken breast, broiled and sliced
1 avocado, peeled, pitted and cubed
1 cup (5 oz/125 g) Cheddar cheese, grated
3 corn tortillas, cut thin and fried crisp

Heat the oil and saute the tortillas with the garlic and cilantro until the tortillas are soft. Add the onion, tomato puree and cumin and cook for 3 minutes, stirring well. Add all the seasonings and the stock, bring to a boil then remove from the heat. Strain and pour back into the skillet. Simmer for 30 minutes. Portion into bowls, top each bowl with chicken, avocado, cheese and tortilla strips.

Cream of Jalapeño Soup

This is a wonderful soup and not at all spicy. It just lets the fruity flavor of the chiles come through. It is vibrant and fresh tasting, allowing each vegetable to give its own distinctive contribution. You'll love it.

The vegetables
2 tbl vegetable oil
1 leek, diced
1 white onion, diced
1 rib celery, diced
1 carrot, diced
2 cloves garlic, finely diced

3 tbl unsalted butter
3 red jalapeños, de-seeded, de-veined and finely diced
2 green jalapeños, de-seeded, de-veined and finely diced

1 tbl all-purpose flour
2 cups (16 fl oz/500 ml) chicken stock
1 cup (8 fl oz/250 ml) white wine
1 tsp thyme
1/2 tsp oregano
1 cup (5 oz/125 g) Cheddar cheese, grated
2 tbl double cream
1 tsp white pepper
1/2 tsp garlic salt
1/2 tsp celery seeds
cilantro leaves for garnish

Over a moderate flame heat the oil. Saute the vegetables until the onion is soft and set aside.

Melt the butter over a moderate heat and saute the jalapeños. Mix in the flour. Add the remaining ingredients, except the veggie mix, and bring to a simmer. Cook for 10 minutes.

Remove from the heat and mix in the veggies.

Allow to cool and blend in your food processor until smooth. Return to your pot and gently heat up. As soon as your soup begins to bubble garnish with cilantro leaves and serve.

If you wish to be cool – south-western style – you could zig-zag cold cream or red chile sauce (see below) over the soup with a squeezy or squirt bottle. Most catering stores sell them these days.

Red Chile Sauce

Dice 2 red bell peppers and combine with 1 diced shallot, 1 diced clove of garlic, 1 diced red chile, 1/4 cup (1 1/4 oz/30 g) diced cilantro and 1/4 cup (2 1/2 fl oz/60 ml) chicken stock. Boil over a high heat for 5 minutes. Pour into a blender, add 1 tbl lime juice and 1/2 tsp celery salt. Puree until smooth.

Strain through a fine sieve and pour into your squirt bottle.

Navy Bean and Collared Green Soup

The navy bean is a kidney bean, occasionally called the pea bean or beautiful bean. It has been a standard food item in the US Navy since 1856 — 'the Army gets the gravy and the Navy gets the beans, beans, beans, beans'.

1 small smoked ham hock
5 cups (2 pints/1 1/4 litres) chicken stock
3 cups (1 lb/450 g) navy or dried white beans – soak in water overnight, boil in fresh water for 20 minutes and then strain
1 white onion, diced
2 clove garlic, diced

2 ribs celery, finely chopped
1 tbl parsley, finely diced
I should now include mashed potatoes, but I can't bring myself to. Play with the idea of mash, if you so desire.
1 tbl Pepper Seasoning (see p. 24)

Boil the ham hock in the stock until soft. Add the rest of the ingedients and cook until you have a thick stew. About 2 hours. You may need extra stock, to ensure the soup doesn't dry out, before all the flavors have blended.

This filling soup used to be served, along with Cuban bread, to the Hispanic cigar workers in The Columbia restaurant, Ybor City, Tampa, Florida. They'd try to eat for a few cents each day in order to send the majority of their pay checks home.

Cuban bread is distinctive for its crisp crust and flattened top. Cuban bakers introduce dampness, to create the crust, by lining brick ovens with banana leaves or by laying palm fronds on top of the loaves. The bread is spread with yellow mustard and filled with thinly sliced roast pork, ham, a salami and a tart cheese.

Acorn Squash Soup with Smoked Chicken

Squash which comes from the genus *cucurbita* includes the pumpkin, gourd and zucchini among its ranks. The acorn squash is my favorite. It has a distinctive nutty flavor and many uses. This special soup is fast and furious and more of a sauteed sauce.

Smoke the chicken yourself if you can. Small smokers are quite easily obtainable.

1 small onion, grated
1 tbl butter
1 clove garlic, finely diced
2 cups (10 oz/250 g) squash, cooked and diced
5 cups (2 pints/1 1/4 litres) chicken stock
1 bay leaf

1 tbl brown sugar
1 tsp Curry Seasoning (see p. 24)
1/2 tsp nutmeg
1 tsp celery salt
1 tsp ground black pepper
1 cup (8 fl oz/250 ml) single cream
1 1/2 cups (8 oz/185 g) smoked chicken, diced

Saute the onion in the butter until soft. Add the garlic and squash, cook for a further 5 minutes – keep stirring.

In a separate pot bring the stock to boil. Add all the remaining ingredients except the chicken and boil for a further 20 minutes. Add the squash mix and simmer for 5 minutes. Turn off the heat and whisk for 2 minutes.

Portion into bowls and top with the chicken. Place the bowls under your grill and brown the tops. Serve immediately.

Roast Tomato Soup with Chipotle Creme Fraiche

Growing tomatoes may seem a rather anal exercise. But I gotta tell you the difference in flavor, compared to that of the store-bought boloney, is huge. If you are lucky, you may find a local organic grower. Not quite chalk and cheese but definitely the difference between three flying ducks and one wooden goose. A chipolte en adobe is a dried smoked jalapeño in tomato sauce.

1 tbl olive oil
10 plum tomatoes, roasted and peeled
1 small onion, finely diced
2 ribs celery, finely diced
2 tbl unsalted butter
1 tbl My General Seasoning (see p. 23)
1 tbl sugar
4 cups (1 ³/₄ pints/1 litre) chicken stock

1 tbl mixed herbs (oregano is a must)
2 medium carrots, cleaned and grated
1 small red bell pepper, de-seeded and finely chopped

For the creme fraiche
1 cup creme fraiche
1 chipotle en adobe, mashed

Mix the oil with the tomatoes.

Saute the onion and celery in the butter for 5 minutes. Add the seasoning and sugar. Cook for a further 5 minutes. Allow to cool.

Bring the stock to boil and add the tomatoes. Cook for 5 minutes.

Allow the soup to cool. Add a the mixed herbs. Mix the onion and celery into the soup. Drop in the carrots and bell pepper. Puree until smooth. Pour back into your pot and bring to a simmer. Keep warm.

Mix together the creme fraiche and mashed chipotle and keep at room temperature in your squeezy bottle. Portion the soup and zig-zag the creme fraiche across the top.

Creamed Corn Chowder with Green Chile Salsa

Corn with chicken and ham is as southern as Vivien Leigh's 18-inch waist. Try to use fresh corn from an early summer harvest, for the best results — even if corn is now available all year round. For a real country flavor, after you have scraped the raw kernels off the cob, boil the 'naked' cobs, in a cup or so of water, for a little corn essence, which you can later add to the chowder. This soup is a good example of how I like to layer my flavors by giving the ingredients a variety of cooking times.

4 cups (1 ³/₄ pints/1 litre) chicken stock
1 tbl My General Seasoning (see p. 23)
1 tsp oregeno
2 bay leaves
1 tbl parsley, finely chopped
1 tsp crushed black peppercorns
4 rashers of streaky bacon, grilled until crispy
1 cup (5 oz/125 g) smoked ham, diced
2 ribs celery, diced

2 small white onions, finely diced – small onions are usually stronger than the large ones
2 carrots, cleaned and finely diced
1 red bell pepper, finely chopped
1 yellow bell pepper, finely chopped
2 cups (10 oz/250 g) roast fresh corn kernels
1 cup (8 fl oz/250 ml) double cream
1 cup (5 oz/125 g) potatoes, diced and parboiled

Bring the stock to the boil and add the seasoning, herbs, peppercorns, bacon and ham. Cook at a simmer for 20 minutes. Add the celery, onion and carrot and cook for 10 more minutes. Add the bell peppers and corn and cook for a further 10 minutes. Take off the heat and mix in the cream and potatoes. Leave for 10 minutes with the lid on.

Portion the soup and serve with my simple Green Chile Salsa (see below).

Green Chile Salsa

Grill 8 green jalapeños, de-seed and dice. Roast 1 white onion until it is nearly black and then dice. Finely dice 1 clove of garlic. Mix together and add 1 tbl of olive oil, ¹/₂ tsp marjoram, ¹/₄ tsp garlic salt and 1 tbl cider vinegar. Keep at room temperature. Adding the oil and vinegar to this simple salsa helps freshen the palate whilst eating the rich chowder.

Chile Stew or 'Bossy in a Bowl'

Kansas City claims to have the best steak and, by extension, of course, the best steak soup. I wouldn't argue. This is a version I adapted from the soup at the city's Plaza III restaurant. I have omitted the frozen vegetables in favor of peppers and subsequently renamed it. 'Bossy', by the way, is an old lunch counter name for the cow.

3 cups (1 lb/450 g) chuck steak, cubed
flour
butter
1 large onion, finely chopped
2 ribs celery, finely diced
2 carrots, chopped
1 tbl olive oil
5 cups (2 pints/1 ¼ litres) beef stock

8 plum tomatoes, roasted, peeled and mashed
1 tbl tomato puree
1 red jalapeño, de-seeded, de-veined and finely diced
1 red bell pepper, roasted, peeled and finely diced
1 tbl My Chili Seasoning (see p. 25)
snipped chives to garnish

Dust the steak with the flour. Heat the butter and quickly saute over a high heat until browned – not burnt.

Saute the onion, celery and carrot together in the oil, until the onion is soft.

Bring the stock to a boil and add all the ingredients, except the beef. Cook for 20 minutes. Add the beef, bring to a simmer and cook for 2 hours or until the meat is fork tender.

Portion and garnish with snipped chives.

Black and White Bean Soup

The visual effect of two different colored soups in one bowl is terrific — you may wish to try it with other combinations. Or maybe even three different soups! I had great success with roast tomato, green chile and white bean — the colors of the Mexican flag — which I once cooked for Cinco de Mayo, Mexican Independence Day.

Black Bean Soup

5 cups (2 pints/1 ¼ litres) chicken stock – for a veggie alternative, use water and leave out the ham later
4 cups (1 ¼ lb/500 g) black beans, soaked overnight, boiled in fresh water for 20 minutes and drained
2 cloves garlic, finely diced

2 white onions, finely diced
2 red bell peppers, roasted, peeled and diced
1 cup (5 oz/125 g) cubed country ham
1 tsp garlic salt
½ tsp coarse-ground black pepper
1 tbl cider vinegar
½ tsp ground cumin

Bring the stock to the boil and add all the ingredients. Cook for 4 hours over a low heat. Keep warm. You may need to keep stirring the bottom of the pan.

White Bean Soup

5 cups (2 pints/1 ¼ litres) chicken stock
1 ½ cups (8 oz/185 g) dry white beans,
soaked overnight, boiled in fresh water for
20 minutes and drained
a 2 lb/900 g ham hock
2 ribs of celery, finely chopped
1 onion, finely chopped
1 green bell pepper, finely chopped
2 bay leaves

1 tbl Jalapeño Tabasco
1 tsp white pepper
1 tsp thyme
1 tsp garlic salt
1 tsp oregano
1 tbl cayenne/chile flakes
½ tsp coarse-ground black pepper

Bring the stock to boil. Add all the other ingredients and cook over a low heat for 4 hours or until the meat begins to fall off the bone. Remove the ham hock. Scrape the meat off and coarsely chop it. Return the meat to the beans and cook for a further 1 hour.

Whichever soup is thickest – it should be the white bean – place in one half of your soup bowl, you may wish to hold the bowl at a slight angle, so as to keep the soup in just one half of the bowl. Quickly ladle in the black bean soup. When they meet they should say 'hi', but not get intimate. Garnish with Jack Cheese and Kenny's French Quarter Seasoning (see p. 21).

> All bean afficionados should check out the McClure Bean Soup Festival in Pennsylvania. There, at the Civil War Memorial, you'll find huge iron kettles, gallons of beans, tons of beef and mountains of crackers.

DRINKS, APPETIZERS & SMALL PLATES

DRINKS

Books on food rarely mention seroius alcohol. Why? They all discuss wine. But I like to have a real drink with my tamales. What follows are my four favorite cocktails. They make great aperitifs or accompaniments to snacks.

The cocktail, of course, is largely an American invention. They've been around since the 19th century but it was in the prohibition era that they really took off as a way to mask the harsh taste of bootleg liquor. Bartenders have been mixing and naming brave new concoctions ever since, from the B–52 to the Zombie.

Margarita

My favorite form of serial self-punishment. A chap called Pancho invented this drink by mistake in the summer of 1942. Serving drinks at Tommy's Place in the town of Juarez, he had been asked to make a Magnolia. Having forgotten the ingredients – gin, lemon juice, cream and grenadine – he instead knocked up a substitute – tequila, lime and Cointreau. Confusing his flowers he called it a Daisy – Margarita in Spanish.

3 lime wedges
Kosher salt on a side plate, for the rim.
1 ¹/₂ fl oz gold tequila – Cuervo Especial

¹/₂ fl oz Cointreau
¹/₄ fl oz Grand Marnier
³/₄ fl oz fresh lime juice

Run a lime wedge around the rim of the glass, then dip in salt. Shake off any excess.

Fill a cocktail shaker with enough ice to fill your glass. Squeeze in the lime wedges, drop them in the shaker. Pour in all the booze and the lime juice. Shake the diablo out of it – for about 30 seconds – and pour all the contents into your glass. Drink. Now repeat, but maybe make some for your guests this time.

The Manhattan

In 1874 a bartender at the Manhatten Club invented this drink to celebrate the election of Governor Samuel Tilden. The recipe varies, but I prefer dry over sweet vermouth

1 ¹/₂ fl oz blended whiskey – Canadian Club
¹/₂ fl oz dry vermouth

dash of Angostura bitters
1 maraschino cherry

Add ice to a mixing glass, pour in the booze and stir. Strain into a martini glass and garnish with the cherry.

Bloody Mary

This recipe is taken from my first book. It is too good to alter. I cannot write the recipe down without thinking of Herman – the gentleman who poured bloodys for me, with his pickled asparagus garnish, at the side bar of Arnauds in New Orleans.

5 cups (2 pints/1.2 litres) Campbells V-8 Juice
1 tbl creamed horseradish
1 tbl coarse-grain mustard
1 tsp Worcestershire sauce

2 tsp Louisiana sauce
1 tbl lemon juice
1 tsp sea salt
1 tsp cayenne
1 tsp coarse-ground black pepper

Mix well and chill overnight. Pour good quality vodka over ice and squeeze a lime quarter into the glass. Pour in the Bloody mix and stir with a celery stick. Leave the celery as garnish.

I personally rim the glass with a cayenne, black pepper and celery salt mix. But this may be a little bit too much for some folk.

Martini

The history and the art of making a classic Martini has been well documented elsewhere. However, there are plenty of wild – some would say heretical – ways to play with this classic concept. As Johnny Carson said, 'Happiness is finding two olives in your martini when you're hungry.' So I suggest you just misbehave.

The Red Light in Chicago makes a frozen mango Martini, which really excites. This drink is similar to a daiquiri but is a Martini none the less. My favorite Martini is the Cajun version, where you steep chiles in the vodka for at least six days. Flavored vodkas are of course everywhere now. Why not produce your own? It's easy. A straightforward process of infusion of anything from chocolate or cinnamon to cilantro or cranberry.

Appetizers

Appetizers are the real winners in restaurants for all concerned. They offer sound profitability for any restaurateur and can be an easy way for the guests to experiment with foodstuffs and dine inexpensively. The Spanish cottoned on to this idea years ago. Here are my favorite small plates. Small, simple and packed with flavor.

The Flour Tortilla

Tortillas were originally made with corn. It was not until the 16th century, when the Spanish arrived in Mexico, that flour was used as an alternative. The flour version is now more commonplace.

Tortillas are very easy to make and can be used as a great substitute for regular bread. It was traditionally a way of carrying a meal into the field — the classic peasant meal to go. These days, it is the basis for an unlimited number of creations.

The merchurial Joachim Splichal of LA's Patina restaurant owns what he calls a 'tacone' stand in the city. He serves vibrantly colored tortillas, rolled into cones and stuffed with wacky ingredients, such as Chinese chicken salad, shredded salmon with sticky rice or jerk shrimp. Get the idea? Get funky!

2 cups (10 oz/250 g) flour, you will need more for coating
1 ½ tsp salt
1 ½ tsp baking powder

5 level tbl vegetable shortening
approx. ¾ cup (6 fl oz/175 ml) warm water

Sift together the dry ingredients. With your fingers crumble in the shortening. Work it in until you have a coarse mix – about 10 minutes.

Add half the water and make into a stiff dough. Knead for 20 seconds. Gradually add most of the rest of the water, and keep working until you have a soft and wet dough.

Divide the dough into 20 small pieces. Form into perfect balls. Cover with cling film and let rest for 10 minutes.

Heat a cast-iron skillet, or your thickest-bottomed pan, to a medium-high heat. Dip each ball in flour to lightly coat, then gently stretch them into 2-inch circles.

Now the rolling bit: on a clean work surface roll them as best you can. Ensure you keep a thin round. With great care transfer them, one at a time, to the dry skillet. Cook for 40 seconds, or until the tortilla begins to bubble. Flip over and cook for a further 10 seconds.

This may sound a real tricky exercise but, it isn't. Making tortillas will take a few attempts to perfect. However, the ingredients are inexpensive and the outcome marvellous.

Stack the tortillas and wrap in a moist linen towel.

Chicken and Papaya Quesadilla with Green Chile Chutney

Bobby Flay's Mesa Grill in New York serves up wonderful bold and sizzling south-western inspired cooking – vibrant flavors and art-on-a-plate presentation. I prefer to present the quesadilla in the Bobby Flay style – sandwich-stacked tortillas – as opposed to the more traditional folded over omelette style. Traditionally quesadilla's were raw flour tortilla sandwiches shallow fried: in less traditional circles it is now more often a cooked tortilla re-grilled.

For each portion you will need two 6-inch tortillas. Lighly sprinkle one side of each tortilla with paprika and warm the seasoned side on a large skillet.

For the filling: dice some roast chicken real small. Mix with finely diced red jalapeños, cilantro leaves and diced papaya. Spread the mix over the unseasoned side of a tortilla. Cover with a sharp, grated cheese and sprinkle sea salt and black pepper over the cheese.

Place the tortilla under the grill and melt the cheese. As soon as this happens, top with another tortilla, seasoned side up. Place under the grill until the tortilla begins to brown.

Place on the chopping board and cut into quarters, roughly keeping the round shape. Place on a plate and centre with the chutney. Garnish with snipped chives.

Green Chile Chutney

2 cups (10 oz/250 g) green jalapenos, coarsely chopped
1 green bell pepper, coarsely chopped
3 tbl fresh ginger, peeled and chopped
1 1/2 cups (8 oz/185 g) raisins

2 1/3 cups (12 oz/295 g) brown sugar
1/2 tsp crushed cloves
salt to taste
1 1/2 cups (12 fl oz/375 ml) cider vinegar

Mix all the ingredients in a saucepan. Over a low heat, simmer until thick. Allow to cool, then transfer to a Mason jar or a similar sealable container. Store in a cool place for 2 days before use.

Eggplant Pirogues with Seafood Gumbo Gravy

We should be looking at another long recipe, the best always are. But, I haven't really got the space, so I'll give you the basics.

After peeling eggplants I carve them into little boats – a pirogue is a flat barge-like affair used on the bayous of Louisiana. I dip the boats in an egg wash and then coat them in seasoned breadcrumbs. The boats are gently fried until crispy. I centre two pirogues on a plate and smother them in the strained juice from seafood gumbo. They taste wonderful. It's an idea I stole from Chef Paul Prudhomme. Check out his 1984 book *Louisiana Kitchen* – a must for anyone interested in American cooking.

Oyster Rockefeller

The recipe is still a sort of secret belonging to the owners and chefs of Antoines, in New Orleans. But we've all eaten enough to achieve similar results. Watercress is the key and certainly not spinach.

Shuck as many oysters as needed. I go for 3 per portion.

Simmer shallots in buttered water until they are limp. Add some watercress, parsley and fennel. Add a little of Kenny's Seafood Seasoning (see p. 21) and remove from the heat as soon as the watercress wilts. Strain the mix and puree. Add a little Pernod. Allow to cool a little.

Cover a baking tray with rock salt, to stop the oysters slipping. Spoon the watercress mix over each oyster and bake until the sauce begins to bubble.

Some folk top the sauce with Parmesan. This looks and tastes fine – but it is not authentic.

Shrimp Patties with Chipotle–herbsaint Butter

I first saw these at the Shrimporee in Arkansas Pass, Texas – where everything, but everything is shrimpy.

Mix one
1 tbl peanut oil
1 small red onion, finely diced
1 small red bell pepper, de-seeded, de-veined and finely diced
1 small yellow bell pepper, de-seeded, de-veined and finely diced
1 red jalapeño, de-seeded, de-veined and finely diced
1 clove garlic, finely diced.

Mix two
1 ½ lb/560 g shrimp – I use uncooked, frozen (obviously fresh is best but ensure you're on the coast, for they spoil real fast), headless, shell on; the size I prefer is 21–25 – that's the number of shrimp to the pound
1 tbl fresh cilantro leaves, coarsely chopped
2 tbl snipped chives
1 tbl chopped fresh thyme
1 tsp soy sauce

Heat the oil and saute the vegetables until the onion is soft. Remove from heat and transfer to a mixing bowl.

Peel and de-vein the shrimp. Then either finely chop or pulse in your mixer. If you chop them you may need to add a beaten egg to the final mix to make sure they stick together.

Combine the shrimp with mix one. Form into 5 oz/125 g burgers and chill, covered, for 20 minutes.

Grill the patties for about 5 minutes – turning once.

I like to serve the shrimp patties on a bed of wilted spinach. Wilted greens are simply seasoned and steamed greens. Maybe serve the patties as they do at Commander's Palace in New Orleans – between two pieces of crusty French bread. But by then it's more of a Po'boy.

Wilted Spinach

1 tbl unsalted butter
½ small red onion, grated
4 slices streaky bacon, fried until crisp and diced
1 tbl cider vinegar
1 tbl white wine

1 tbl double cream
9 cups (3 lb/1.3 kg) washed and picked spinach – not baby
pinch of garlic salt
big pinch of cayenne pepper
big pinch of coarse-ground black pepper

Heat the butter, and, as it melts, add the onion. Saute for 3 minutes. Add all the other ingredients, except the spinach and seasoning. Saute for a further 3 minutes. Take off the heat and fold in the spinach and seasoning. Reaching the desired 'wilt' will take 4 minutes.

We want a shiny, soft result. Centre the spinach, place one patty on the spinach and top with my Chipotle-herbsaint butter (see below). Easy.

Chipotle-herbsaint Butter

Bring some unsalted butter to a softened state. Mix in a little chipotle (dried and smoked jalapeños) and flavor with Herbsaint. Herbsaint is an anise-flavored liquor. You may wish to use Ricard or Pernod.

Wild Mushroom Quesadilla with Corn Salsa

This is a faster version of the previous quesadilla (see p. 87). Simply saute some diced wild mushrooms in butter. Add a little soy sauce and Cheddar cheese. Allow the cheese to melt and then sprinkle with My General Seasoning (see p. 23).

Warm your tortilla and then cover with a layer of the mushroom mix. Fold in half and brown each side. Cut into thirds and serve. Maybe centre the plate with my Roast Corn Salsa (see p. 18) – I do.

Crab Empanaditas with Rocket Salad and Mustard Oil

Empanadas are fried pastry turnovers of Mexican origin and are not dissimilar to British Cornish pasties. In Spanish *empanar* means to 'bake in pastry'. Empanaditas are baby versions of empanadas. Ideally, the flour to use is Masa Harina – the staple Hispanic–American maize flour. Traditionally they are stuffed with pork or picadillo (see my picadillo recipe on page 95), but I love the crab version. What you choose for a filling is limited only by your imagination.

DRINKS, APPETIZERS AND SMALL PLATES

For the dough
2 cups (10 oz/250 g) all-purpose flour or
Masa Harina
1 tsp salt
1 tsp sugar
1/2 tsp garlic salt

1/2 tsp coarse-ground black pepper
5 tbl vegetable shortening
1 egg, beaten
1/3 cup (3 fl oz/75 ml) dry white wine
1 tbl snipped chives

Sift the dry ingredients. With your fingers thoroughly mix in the shortening until the mix resembles cornmeal. Add the egg, wine and chives and knead until the dough is soft.

On a floured clean counter roll out the dough to about 1/8 inch thickness. Using a 3-inch cookie cutter cut out circles. Those bits left over should be rolled up and flattened, to be cut again. Refrigerate the pastry circles. Do not stack them.

For the filling
1/2 cup (4 fl oz/125 ml) olive oil
1 white onion, grated
1 red onion, grated
4 cloves garlic, diced

2 plum tomatoes, roasted, peeled and pureed
2 cups (10 oz/250 g) fresh picked crabmeat
2 red jalapeños, de-seeded, de-veined and
finely diced
1 tbl Kenny's Seafood Seasoning (see p. 21)

Combine the ingredients for the filling and put to one side.

Lightly brush the pastry circles with water. Place a spoonful of the mix in the centre and fold the circle into a half-moon shape – your turnover. Pinch the edges with a fork.

Heat 2 inches of peanut oil in a skillet to 350°F/180°C/gas mark 4. Without crowding, fry the empanaditas until golden brown, turning once or twice. Drain on kitchen towels.

Rocket Salad

Rocket is actually a green called arugula. It has been popular since Roman times. Being a member of the mustard family, it has a delicate spicy, peppery flavor, and I find it a great help when a plate is in need of color or height. Just make sure you buy young leaves.

For the salad
3 cups (1 lb/450 g) rocket
1 red bell pepper, cored and finely diced
1 small yellow bell pepper, cored and finely diced
3 stalks chives, snipped
1 small red onion, halved and sliced
1 red jalapeño, de-seeded, de-veined and finely diced
2 tbl cilantro leaves, just picked off the stalks

For the dressing
1 shallot, minced
1 tsp Dijon mustard
1 tbl rice wine vinegar
1 tbl fresh lemon juice
salt and pepper to taste
4 tbl olive oil

For the mustard oil
2 tbl black mustard seeds
3 cloves garlic, diced
1 red jalapeño de-seeded, de-veined and finely diced
1 tbl snipped chives
1 small yellow bell pepper, cored, de-veined and finely diced
1 tbl white wine vinegar
½ cup (4 fl oz/125 ml) olive oil

Combine all salad ingredients and chill for 10 minutes. Combine the dressing ingredients and set aside. Combine the mustard oil ingredients.

To serve: toss together the dressing and the rocket salad and arrange in the middle of the plate. Drizzle the mustard oil around the plate and lean two hot empanaditas against the salad. Serve immediately before the heat destroys the rocket.

Rock Shrimp Hash

Allen Susser, owner of Chef Allen's in North Miami, is a star of the new Floridian cooking style which mixes Caribbean and southern cooking. One of his recipes inspired the following dish. Rock shrimp are the finest shrimp on our planet. Thankfully a machine was invented in 1988 to shell them. If you have ever seen them in their 'happy house' state you would understand. The hash sits on a sweet potato pancake.

For the pancake
3 tbl olive oil
*1 12oz/300 g yam or sweet potato, peeled,
boiled and mashed*
½ tbl My General Seasoning (see p. 23)
2 eggs, beaten
½ cup (4 fl oz/125 ml) milk
all-purpose flour

For the hash
1 tbl olive oil
½ red onion, diced

1 yellow tomato, cored and finely diced
*1 small green bell pepper, cored and finely
diced*
*1 red jalapeño, de-seeded, de-veined and
finely diced*
½ clove garlic, diced
*2 ⅓ cup (12 oz/300 g) rock (or any other
fresh) shrimp, diced*
1 tbl white wine
1 tsp thyme
1 tbl cilantro leaves, coarsely chopped
1 tsp Pepper Seasoning (see p. 24)

To make the pancake: beat the oil into the potato. Add the seasoning and mix thoroughly. Beat in the eggs, then mix in the milk. Add enough flour for the mix to hold together. Form into 3-inch patties and flatten. Chill.

Heat the oil to medium temperature. Add the onion, tomato, bell pepper, jalapeño and garlic. Saute for 5 minutes and keep stirring. Add the shrimp, wine and herbs and cook for 2 minutes. Take off the heat and mix in the seasoning. Let it sit now for a few minutes then spoon over the pancakes.

Turkey Picadillo with Hot Tomato Rum Down Sauce

Piccadillo (pronounced 'pick-a-DE-yo') is a mincemeat stew-like affair found in the south-west – the name derived from the Spanish word *picar* – to cut into small pieces. In Cuba it's a lunch-counter favorite. The turkey is native to North America and plays a huge part in American history (Benjamin Franklin wanted it as the national emblem instead of the bald eagle). Anyways I love this dish. It is probably one of the best ways to cook turkey. Why not try it as an alternative Thanksgiving dish?

3 cups (1 lb/450 g) ground turkey
1 tsp ground cumin
1 tsp garlic salt
1 tsp coarse-ground black pepper
¼ tsp crushed cloves
1 tbl olive oil
3 cloves garlic, diced
1 small white onion, diced
½ red bell pepper, de-seeded, de-veined and finely chopped

1 small tomato, cored and finely chopped
10 pimento-stuffed green olives, finely chopped
¼ cup (1 ¼ oz/30 g) raisins (optional – I would leave them out)
1 tbl capers
½ cup (4 fl oz/125 ml) dry white wine
1 tbl tomato puree

In a large mixing bowl crumble the turkey and mix well with the cumin, salt, pepper and cloves. In a skillet, heat the oil to a medium temperature. Add the garlic, onion and bell pepper. Cook until the onion is soft – 5 minutes.

Stir in the tomato and cook for a further two minutes. Add the turkey mixture and mix in well, but keep stirring. After a few minutes add the olives, raisins and capers and cook for a further 2 minutes.

Stir in the wine and tomato puree. Lower the heat and cook until the wine has evaporated – about 8 minutes. We need a moist but not soupy mixture. Taste for seasoning and serve immediately. Picadillo does keep, but I feel it is best used straight after cooking as the cumin can sometimes become overpowering.

Some folk like to turn their picadillo into a meat loaf. This is bit of a shame. It should, as tradition says, be served with black beans, white rice, Cuban-style deep-fried eggs and fried plantains. You may wish to change the type of meat to suit your own tastes.

BIG PLATES AND DINNER SALADS

BIG PLATES

Catfish Tacos with Tequila Creamed Corn

This is a wonderful, unholy alliance of Cajun and Mexican influences. Taco is a Mexican–Spanish word meaning 'wad' or 'plug'. The taco we normally see is the U-shaped crisp corn tortilla plugged with a filling. Here I use a flour tortilla instead to make the result more pliable. Catfish is the fifth most popular fish consumed in the US. It is a spiny, scaleless fish, and tastes like the best wild trout.

1 tbl olive oil
1 small red onion, finely diced
1 rib celery, finely diced
1 small red jalapeño, de-seeded, de-veined and finely diced
1 clove garlic, diced
3 tbl Kenny's Seafood Seasoning (see p. 21)
5 rashers streaky bacon, diced and fried until crisp
2 tbl double cream

3 tbl white wine
1 tbl unsalted butter
2 8 oz/185 g skinless catfish fillets (or any strong flavored freshwater fish e.g. trout), diced into 1.5cm (¹/₂ in) cubes
1 tsp tomato puree
8 6-inch flour tortillas

Over a medium heat warm the oil and saute the onion, celery, jalapeño and garlic until the onion is soft. Take off the heat and add half the seasoning. Mix in and add the bacon. Return to the heat and mix in the cream, wine and butter. When the sauce begins to bubble add the fish, tomato puree and the rest of the seasoning. Cook for 4 minutes. Remove from the heat and keep warm.

In a skillet big enough to hold a tortilla heat a little olive oil and brown on both sides. Gently remove the tortilla from the skillet. Fold into your U shape. Place two beer cans on your work surface and press a taco in between. Keep repeating, until all the tacos are made. Now let them cool.

How you present the dish is up to you. I always use guacamole to stop my tortillas slipping. You may just want to lay them against each other. Fill each taco with your catfish mix. Place on your plate and garnish with snipped chives and Kenny's French Quarter Seasoning (see p. 22). Surround with the corn sauce. I like the juices from the catfish to run into the sauce.

Tequila Creamed Corn

2 tbl unsalted butter
2 scallion stalks, diced
1 clove garlic, finely minced
1 small white onion, finely diced
2 poblano chiles, roasted, peeled, de-seeded and diced
1 cup (5 oz/125 g) roast corn kernels
1 red jalapeño, de-seeded, de-veined and finely diced

1 yellow bell pepper, roasted, cored and diced
1/2 cup (4 fl oz/125 ml) chicken stock
1/2 cup (2 1/2 oz/60 g) cilantro leaves, chopped
1 tbl white wine
1 tbl double cream
2 tbl gold tequila

Melt the butter and saute the scallions, garlic, onion and poblanos until the onion is soft. Add the corn, jalapeño and bell pepper. Cook for 5 more minutes.

In a separate pot heat the stock with the cilantro. Bring to a simmer and add the wine. When bubbles appear again, add the cream and tequila. Keep warm until serving. A sauce this fresh does not need seasoning, although a little black pepper will not go amiss.

Blackened Red Drum with Toasted Pecan Butter and Peach-Tasso Chutney

Chef Paul Prudhomme invented the idea of blackening around 1982. Blackening is the process of coating your meat in herbs and spices and then searing it on a white-hot skillet. This seals in all the juices and flavor. Give it a try, my way – it is nothing like the dull executions you find on the high street. The accompaniments are mine, but they still play with all the inherent Louisiana flavors and are authentic. If you can't find red drum try grey mullet or hake.

4 8 oz/185 g red drum fillets, 2 inches thick   *2 tbl unsalted butter*
6 tbl My Blackening Seasoning (see p. 22)

Blackening is a very quick and intense process so before you begin make sure everything is in place. Heat your thickest skillet until it is very hot. Remove to another part of the stove and allow to cool slightly. Coat the fillets in the seasoning. Drop the butter in the skillet. (I hope you had your sleeves rolled down!) Immediately add the fillets. After 2 minutes flip them over and return to the heat. Cook for a further 3 minutes, then remove to a warm plate. Don't worry, the fish keep cooking.

Assemble the dish. Centre a 4-inch round of the chutney (see below) on the plate. Top with a fillet and place a tablespoon of the butter on top of the fillet. Leave for 1 minute then serve.

Toasted Pecan Butter

¹/₃ cup (2 oz/45 g) pecans   *¹/₄ cup (2 ¹/₂ fl oz/60 ml) honey*
¹/₂ cup (2 ¹/₂ oz/60 g) unsalted butter,
softened

Pre-heat oven to 300°F/150°C/gas mark 2. Spread the pecans out on a roasting pan and place in the oven for 10 minutes. Remove from the oven, allow to cool then finely chop. In a small bowl beat the butter to a smooth consistency. Add the honey, stir in the pecans and mix well. Refrigerate until needed. Allow to reach room temperature before using.

Peach-Tasso Chutney

Tasso is a spicy smoked ham from Louisiana, if you can't find it use crispy bacon or smoked ham instead.

1 cup (8 fl oz/250 ml) cider vinegar
2 tbl brown sugar
2 lemons, grated and juiced
1 tsp ground ginger
1 stick cinnamon
¼ tsp ground coriander
pinch of cloves

pinch of cayenne
1 cup (5 oz/125 g) white onion, finely diced
⅓ cup (2 oz/45 g) Tasso
¾ cup (3 ¾ oz/90 g) tinned peaches, strained and diced

Combine the vinegar and sugar in a saucepan. Bring to a boil. Add the remaining ingredients and reduce to half. Lower the heat and simmer for 5-10 minutes until thick. Remove the cinnamon stick and allow to cool. Keep stirring. Chill for 4 hours or more.

Pecan-crusted Pan-fried Trout with Jalapeño-Chive Oil

Richard Brautigan, author of *Trout Fishing in America*, describes trout as being precious and like an intelligent metal. In my opinion his zany writing is streets ahead of Burroughs and Kerouac.

Anyways, going fishing and cooking your own catch is one reason why we are on this planet. It is a true experience. This is my own dish, one I have cooked for years.

4 trout fillets
Kenny's Seafood Seasoning (see p. 21)
½ cup (4 fl oz/125 ml) Dijon mustard
2 tbl maple syrup
3 cloves garlic, diced
1 tsp fresh oregano

1 tbl cilantro leaves, finely chopped
1 tbl olive oil
1 tsp garlic salt
1 tsp cayenne pepper
1 tsp soy sauce
2 cups (10 oz/250 g) pecans, crushed

Make sure all bones are pinned out of the fillets. Dust the fish with the seasoning and refrigerate until everything else is ready.

Pre-heat the oven to 375°F/190°C/gas mark 5. Combine all the remaining ingredients. Grease your baking tray. Lay the fillets down and top with the pecan mix. Cook for 10 minutes then transfer to another baking tray, greasing it first of course. Changing trays keeps the fish a little cooler underneath. Top with all the pecan mix which fell off the first time. Place under your broiler at a medium heat for 2 minutes and then serve.

Place your chosen accompaniment (see below) in the centre of the plate. Surround with the jalapeño oil and top with the fish. I like to top each fish with sweet potato confetti (see p. 65). Then step back and marvel as your guests enjoy.

Jalapeño-Chive Oil

1 cup (8 fl oz/250 ml) olive oil
1 tbl cider vinegar
1 red jalapeño, de-veined, de-seeded and finely diced
1 small red bell pepper, cored, de-veined and finely diced

1 small yellow bell pepper, cored, de-veined and finely diced
3 chive stalks, finely snipped
½ tsp coarse-ground black pepper
½ tsp celery salt

Combine all ingredients and keep in a dark cupboard for at least 1 day.

Side Orders

The following are a few of my favorite main course side dishes —
delights I've discovered across the States, anywhere from taco
shacks to celebrated temples.

Potato Chips with Maytag Blue Cheese – I first tasted these at the Buckhead Diner in
Atlanta, Georgia. My potato chips are thinly sliced Kennebec potatoes, deep-fried in fresh
groundnut oil, drained and dusted in Kenny's French Quarter Seasoning (see p. 22). Maytag
cheese is a smooth blue cheese from Iowa. It's made from the milk of Holstein-Friesian
cows. Melt the cheese over the warm chips. If you can't find Maytag, maybe just use your
favorite blue cheese.

Greek Salad from the Hyde Park Chop House in Moreland Heights, Cleveland, Ohio.
(Cleveland, to me, is one confusing city.) Somewhat *passé*, but to me this is a truly refreshing
classic. Make it with real cold iceberg and endive lettuce, tomatoes, feta cheese, olives,
scallions and anchovies

Chile Verde is the signature dish at the busy Red Iguana in Salt Lake City. The place is a real
dive, but how can anyone ignore a restaurant which serves ten different types of mole.
Mole (a Nahuatl word meaning 'mixture') is a spicy sauce containing chiles and chocolate.
Chocolate, a well-used Latin-American ingredient, gives a velvet smoothness to sauces. Most
folk associate mole with chocolate, but in fact it doesn't have to contain chocolate. My Chile
Verde is a salsa fresca made with tomatillos and green jalapeños – one I quickly saute and
then strain.

Grilled Blue Fish with Island Sherry Sauce

The blue fish is a warm water fish found all the way from the Gulf of Mexico to Maine. It has been labelled 'the bulldog of the sea', due to its ferocious appetite. For certain, nearly every one I have gutted has been stuffed with small fish. The feeding frenzy of the blue fish has no parallel in the marine world. Not even sharks are as destructive.

The problem with 'blues', as with other fast-swimming pelagic species, such as mackerel and tuna, is that the meat spoils quickly because their digestive enzymes are extremely powerful. However, if you are lucky enough to catch them yourself or find yourself at a seaside restaurant offering them, you are in for a real treat. If they don't sell blue fish at the end of your local pier try any strong-textured, oily fish – king fish, wahoo or a small tuna.

For the Island Sherry Sauce
6 plum tomatoes, roasted cored and diced
1 medium white onion, diced
1 mango, peeled, pitted and diced
2 tbl sugar
1 tbl cider vinegar
1 tbl raisins
1 tbl tamarind pulp
1 tsp garlic salt

2 red jalapeños, de-seeded, de-veined and diced
1/2 tsp ground ginger
1/2 tsp nutmeg
1 tbl cilantro leaves, chopped
pinch of cumin
1 tsp paprika
1/2 tsp crushed celery seeds

Saute the tomatoes, onion and mango in the oil until the onion is soft. Add the other sauce ingredients and remove from heat. Allow to cool. Puree and transfer to a sealed container. The sauce will keep for months.

Brush the fish with olive oil, dust with Kenny's French Quarter Seasoning (see p. 22) and broil.

Zig-zag the sauce over the plate. Centre the plate with dressed lettuce leaves and top with the fish.

Chicken Marbella

The Silver Palate is New York's finest and most famous take-out foodie store. It has been around since the summer of 1977 and still serves gloriously simple food. The first time I went in search of this deli, I went on foot. By the time I had reached 110th Street I realized, judging by the neighborhood, that I had walked too far. I rode a cab back — fast!

Chicken Marbella was the first main-course dish offered by the Silver Palate owners Sheila Lukins and Julee Rosso. They insist the marinade needs at least 8 hours to work. I love eating this meal with buttered noodles and a cold bottle of Samuel Adams.

For the marinade
1 cup (5 oz/125 g) pitted prunes
½ cup (2 ½ oz/60 g) pitted green olives
½ cup (2 ½ oz/60 g) capers, drained
½ cup (4 fl oz/125 ml) olive oil
½ cup (4 fl oz/125 ml) red wine vinegar
1 small head of garlic, minced
1 tbl oregano
salt and pepper to taste

1 2 ½-3 lb/1.1-1.3 kg chicken, cut into tenths
2 tbl brown sugar
1 cup (8 fl oz/250 ml) white wine
¼ cup (1 ¼ oz/30 g) fresh cilantro leaves, coarsely chopped

Mix the prunes, olives, capers, olive oil, vinegar, garlic and oregano. Season to taste. Place the chicken in a shallow casserole pan. Pour the marinade over and refrigerate overnight.

Next day: heat oven to 350°F/180°C/gas mark 4. Sprinkle the chicken with brown sugar and pour the wine around the chicken, avoiding washing the sugar off. Place in the oven and cook for 50-60 minutes. After about 20 minutes begin to baste every 10 minutes. To check if the chicken is fully cooked, pierce the thickest parts with a skewer and yellow juices should run out.

Transfer to a serving dish with a slotted spoon. Ladle over a little of the juices, reserving the rest to be passed around in a gravy boat. Sprinkle with cilantro.

Broiled Tautog with Curried Oysters and Apple-Bacon Chutney

Chef Norman Van Aken's cooking was the main reason I first wanted to travel to Key West, Florida. (My copy of his book *Feast of Sunlight* has more food stains than my own work apron.) He was cooking at Louie's Backyard restaurant and I had to try his food. I was not disappointed.

Norman is currently at his own restaurant, Norman's in Coral Gables, Florida. Certain items from his menu inspired my dish. He cooks a Thai Red Curry with Shrimp and Asian Vegetables, Mango Habanero Chutney and Grilled Spice Crusted Chilean Sea Bass. All awesome. But my own dish is a hard act to beat. Tautog is often marketed as blackfish – a member of the wrasse family. This means its meat will be firm and sweet-tasting. A good substitute is snapper, grouper or a big red mullet. You need to make the chutney at least a day in advance.

For the Apple-Bacon Chutney
1 medium white onion, diced
2 tbl peanut oil
2 tsp oregano
2 anaheim chiles or 1 green jalapeño,
de-seeded, de-veined and finely diced
1 poblano chile, or, if you use jalapeños
1 green bell pepper, de-seeded, de-veined
and diced
1 red jalapeño, roasted, de-seeded,
de-veined and diced
½ cup (4 fl oz/125 ml) cider vinegar
1 cup (8 fl oz/250 ml) apple juice
1 cup (8 fl oz/250 ml) cider
2 tbl sugar
3 Granny Smith apples, peeled, cored and
diced into small chunks
4 rashers of streaky bacon, trimmed of any
rind, diced and fried until crispy

16 oysters (4 per plate)
peanut oil
2 limes
4 8 oz/185 g fish fillets

Batter for 16 oysters
2 eggs, beaten
1 ¼ cups (10 fl oz/300 ml) milk
pinch of sea salt
2 twists of black pepper shaker
pinch of cayenne pepper

Coating for 16 oysters
2 cups (10 oz/250 g) cornmeal
1 tsp sugar
1 tsp snipped chives
1 tsp paprika
1 tbl Curry Seasoning (see p. 24)

For the chutney: over a moderate heat saute the onion in the oil until soft – about 6 minutes. Add the oregano and chiles, cook for a further 5 minutes, then pour in the liquids and stir and scrape well. Now add the sugar and apples, cook until the apple is soft but not mushy. Take off the heat and stir in the bacon. Allow to cool and then store in an airtight container for 1 day. The chutney will last for a couple of weeks in the refrigerator.

Combine the batter ingredients and keep mixture chilled before use. Combine the coating ingredients in a medium-sized bowl ready for use. Always keeping one hand dry and one wet, dip the oysters in the batter then the dry mix and place on the side of a plate ready for frying. Meanwhile heat an inch of peanut oil to 350°F/180°C. Shallow fry until crispy. Remember not to crowd them. Keep warm.

Squeeze lime juice over your fish and broil.

I like to serve the oysters in pools of lemon butter at 12, 3, 6 and 9 o'clock on the plate. Lemon butter is simply lemon juice, butter, cream and white wine heated until it bubbles. Place the fish in the middle of the plate and top with the chutney. Garnish with a scattering of snipped chives.

Macadamia-crusted Mahi-Mahi with Tamarind Sauce and Tomato-Tartar Sauce

The presentation of this dish is a little steal from Yellow in Dallas. They present a wonderful creation described as 'a pyramid of Atlantic swordfish with red pepper coulis and ancho cream'.

The Macadamia nut is a seed of the tropical tree indigenous to Australia. It is now a hugely important crop for Hawaii too. (A place where the locals have an uncanny relationship with seafood.) I always crush my nuts with a little olive oil, then keep them at room temperature.

Mahi-Mahi is lean and sweet and should be available from a good fishmonger.

4 8 oz/185 g fish fillets
Kenny's French Quarter Seasoning (see p. 22)

For the Tomato-Tartar Sauce
3 tbl onion juice – grate 1 onion, reserve the juice and use the pulp for another recipe.
1 cup (8 fl oz/250 ml) mayonnaise
2 tbl dill pickle, finely diced
2 tsp fresh lime juice

1 tbl dill weed, finely chopped
1 egg, hard-boiled and grated
4 Roma tomatoes, roasted, peeled, cored and chopped
1 tbl parsley, finely chopped

For the Tamarind Sauce
1 tbl tamarind pulp
1 cup (8 fl oz/250 ml) Salsa Fresca (see p. 15)
1 tbl cider vinegar

Mix all the ingredients for the tomato-tartar sauce together and chill for an hour before use.

For the tamarind sauce mix some tamarind pulp or bottled tamarind sauce with the Salsa Fresca then stir in some cider vinegar. (Tamarind pulp is available from Asian stores.)

For each portion of fish cut the fillet into three equal slices, dust with Kenny's French Quarter Seasoning, and broil over a high heat. Spread the tamarind sauce liberally around the middle of the plate. Centre a large spoon of the tartar sauce and place the fillets around the sauce. I, personally, like to smother the fillets in chopped rocket before arranging them on the plate.

My Brother's Chicken Cacciatore

This dish, I am embarrassed to admit, started me out on my culinary odyssey. Whiskey with chicken? Why not? That's what I say now. *The Joy of Cooking* – the US culinary bible – was published in 1931. Written by Irma S. Rombauer and her reclusive daughter, Marion Rombauer Becker, it reads like a modern book even today. Their cacciatore or 'hunter's' chicken uses brandy and is served over pasta. Following my brother's reinvention, I believe whiskey works fine. Rice is my preferred accompaniment.

a 3 lb/1.3 kg chicken, cut into tenths
½ cup (2 ½ oz/60 g) all-purpose flour
2 tbl peanut oil
2 cups (16 fl oz/500 ml) chicken stock
½ cup (4 fl oz/125 ml) whiskey
½ cup (4 fl oz/125 ml) white wine
1 small red onion, finely chopped
2 cloves garlic, finely diced
2 scallion stalks, chopped
2 cups (10 oz/250 g) tinned plum tomatoes, crushed

½ cup (4 fl oz/125 ml) tomato puree
1 tsp celery salt
1 tsp ground white pepper
2 bay leaves
½ tsp dried thyme
½ tsp oregano
½ tsp marjoram
2 cups (10 oz/250 g) cooked rice, kept warm
snipped chives for garnish
2 cups (10 oz/250 g) button mushrooms, coarsely chopped

Preheat the oven to 425°F/220°C/gas mark 7. Roll the chicken in the flour until completely covered. Heat the oil over a moderate heat. Add the chicken pieces, without crowding, and brown. Remove the chicken and deglaze the pan with a little of the chicken stock, whiskey and wine.

Add the onion, garlic and scallions and saute until the onion is soft. Transfer to a larger skillet if necessary, and, with the exception of the mushrooms, add all the remaining ingredients, including the rest of the whiskey, wine and stock. Mix well. Simmer for 10 minutes.

Transfer to a casserole dish. Add the mushrooms and chicken. We want the chicken settled on top. Bake for 45 minutes. Remove from the oven and turn off the heat. With a slotted spoon remove the chicken to a baking tray. Place the chicken back in the oven for 20 minutes. Keep the sauce warm, but you may need to keep stirring.

Plate your rice. Top with the chicken and smother with your 'hunter's' sauce. Garnish with the chives. And 'la-de-dah', you have my brother's dish.

This recipe also works well with rabbit. But guys, remember, if you are joining in the spring rabbit hunt in Cochiti Pueblo in the south-western states and a girl beats you running for the same rabbit – you must wear her dress until you kill your own rabbit.

Stumptown Stew

Portland, Oregon was given the nickname Stumptown because of the numerous tree stumps that lined the banks of the Willamette river. The stumps remained for years after the city was founded.

The stew was based on the extremely popular beef eaten by the early settlers. The *Oregon Journal* in 1933 reported, 'Even during the days of the Indian uprisings, it is probably a fact that the settlers in the Willamette valley were in much more imminent danger of sudden death on the horns of their cattle than at the tomahawks of the Indians.' You have to appreciate that they were desperate for some meat, after all the salmon they had to eat. Salmon was rather plentiful.

½ oz dried porcini or ceps – or as they're called in Oregan 'boletus'
2 cups (16 fl oz/500 ml) beef stock
1 tbl peanut oil
1 tbl olive oil
1 large onion, coarsely diced
2 cloves garlic, finely diced
½ cup (2 ½ oz/60 g) flour
1 tsp celery salt

½ tsp coarse-ground black pepper
1 tsp thyme
6 cups (2 lb/900 g) chuck steak, cut into 2.5cm (1 in) cubes
2 tbl butter
1 ¾ cups (8 oz/185 g) button mushrooms, thickly sliced
½ cup (4 fl oz/125 ml) Cabernet Sauvignon
1 tbl Worcestershire sauce

Pre-heat the oven to 350°F/180°C/gas mark 4. Soak the dried mushrooms in a ½ cup (4 fl oz/125 ml) of the beef stock for 1 hour.

Pour both oils into a large ovenproof pot, add the onion and garlic and lightly brown over a medium heat. Sift the flour, salt and pepper together. Add the thyme. Dredge the meat in the seasoned flour and then brown in the onion oil.

Melt the butter and saute the button mushrooms until they become soft. Add the sauteed mushrooms, wine, Worcestershire sauce and remaining stock to the meat. Mix well and cover. Bake for 1 ¾ hours

I love serving meat stews with orzo – the pasta that looks like rice. Cook it in chicken stock with chives and diced garlic. On the side I like a salad, preferably of the Caesar variety.

The Zenon Cafe in Eugene, Oregon, produces a neat version with tomato wedges, smoked salmon and steamed asparagus. But I guess the plan is to just play with your favorite ideas.

If you are ever in the north-west you may find it difficult happening upon a satisfying meal. This is simply because the area is so expansive. One place I wholeheartedly recommend you check out – although it may seem I'm ignoring the local cuisine – is 'Esparza's Tex-Mex Restaurant' on Aukeng Street in Portland. Home-smoked meats, fried cactus and glorious brisket are among the delights of this busy and noisy joint.

Blackened Chicken Salad with Molasses–Buttermilk Dressing

Blackening I've already explained (see p. 100). Molasses is a sweetener made from refined sugar, including cane sugar, sugar beets and sometimes sweet potatoes. (If you can't find it use maple syrup.) Molasses was an important trading product in the early colonies. It makes a great dressing.

For the salad

1 head of endive

1 head of oak leaf

2 handfuls of rocket.

1 handful of baby spinach

1 small red bell pepper, cored and finely diced

1 small yellow bell pepper, cored and finely diced

1 red jalapeño, de-seeded, de-veined and finely diced

1 cup (5 oz/125 g) zucchini, finely chopped

2 tbl snipped chives

For the dressing

¼ cup (2 ½ fl oz/60 ml) molasses

½ cup (4 fl oz/125 ml) honey

¼ cup (2 ½ fl oz/60 ml) olive oil

½ cup (4 fl oz/125 ml) buttermilk

2 tbl orange juice

2 tbl cider vinegar

1 tbl lemon juice

½ tsp red jalapeño, de-seeded, de-veined and finely diced

½ tsp celery salt

4 chicken supremes – a chicken 'sue-premm' is the chicken breast, removed when raw

2 tbl My Blackening Seasoning (see p. 22)

Combine all the salad ingredients. Then mix all the dressing ingredients and keep at room temperature.

Blacken the chicken (see p. 100). Once cooked, allow the chicken to sit for a few minutes before slicing to open it out in to a fan-shaped piece of chicken. While the chicken is cooling toss the salad in the dressing and centre in the middle of four plates. Arrange your slices of chicken supreme and sprinkle snipped chives around the whole plate.

Ham Succotash with Cheddar– Jalapeño Bisquits

Succotash comes from the Narraganset Indian word *misickquatash*, which refers to various items, primarily corn, in a pot. More simply, it means whatever you have on hand, depending on the season.

A pioneer ethnographer from Pennsylvannia, Frank Hamilton Cushing, praised succotash in his 1884 book *Zuni Breadstuff*, primarily for its melting pot homogeneity. Today, with people not really understanding what the dish is, the word has began to take on new meanings. Yosemite Sam, in the Looney Tunes cartoons, blasphemed 'Suffering succotash!' and President Reagan used 'South succotash' as an epithet for an out-of-the-way, insignificant small town. Bizarre. The dish is a real treat. Biscuits, or bisquits as they call them in the south, are a regular accompaniment to stews. They are not unlike little soda bread scones and can be prepared on their own and eaten with a flavored butter.

6 cups (2 ½ pints/1.5 litres) chicken stock
1 lb/450 g smoked ham hock, meat cubed
2 tbl unsalted butter
1 white onion, sliced
1 clove garlic, minced
4 oregano leaves, crushed
½ tsp garlic salt
½ tsp coarse-ground black pepper
2 cups (10 oz/250 g) green beans, topped and tailed
2 small yellow zucchini, sliced

3 ears of fresh corn, shucked, roasted and the kernels cut off
4 scallions, chopped
¼ cup (1 ¼ oz/30 g) sunflower seeds, shelled and crushed
½ cup (4 fl oz/125 ml) single cream
½ cup (4 fl oz/125 ml) white wine
1 tbl snipped chives

Bring half the stock to a simmer and add the ham. Cook for 10 minutes. Then heat the butter in a pan and saute the onion and garlic until the onion is soft. Add to the ham stock along with the oregano, garlic salt and pepper.

Pre-heat the oven to 425°F/220°C/gas mark 7. Mix the green beans, zucchini and corn together, then add to the stock mix. Pour into a casserole dish and place in the oven for 20 minutes. Remove from the oven.

Mix in the remaining stock, the scallions and the sunflower seeds. Return to the oven for 30 minutes. Remove again and add the cream, white wine and chives. Mix well. Return to the oven, lower the temperature to 375°F/190°C/gas mark 5 and cook for 45 minutes.

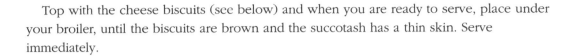

Top with the cheese biscuits (see below) and when you are ready to serve, place under your broiler, until the biscuits are brown and the succotash has a thin skin. Serve immediately.

Cheddar–Jalapeño Bisquits

2 cups (10 oz/250 g) all-purpose flour
1/4 tsp baking soda
1 tbl baking powder
1 tsp salt
6 tbl lard
1 cup (8 fl oz/250 ml) buttermilk

1 cup (5 oz/125 g) sharp Cheddar cheese, grated
1/2 cup Parmesan cheese, grated
1 tbl green jalapeño, de-seeded, de-veined and finely diced

Sift the dry ingredients into a mixing bowl. Cut in the lard until the mixture is like coarse cornmeal. Add the buttermilk and mix to a light dough with your hands. Add the cheeses and jalapeño. If the dough is too sticky add a little more flour and knead in. Wrap your dough in cling film and chill for 20 minutes.

Pre-heat the oven to 450°F/230°C/gas mark 8. Then, on a floured surface, roll the dough out to a 1/2-inch thickness. Cut into your favorite size – which I know is 1 1/2 inches. On a floured baking tray, bake your bisquits for 10-12 minutes until lightly golden.

Jambalaya Cakes with Sauteed Crawfish and Old-fashioned Tomato Sauce

If we view America as a melting pot nation then this has to be the definitive melting pot dish. The 'jamba' comes from the old Spanish (or French) for ham, 'a la' is French and 'ya' is slave talk for 'rice'. No one is too sure of its real origins, but it was created on the plantations many years ago. Although similar to paella in execution, it is one of the few authentically American dishes. This is my new twist on the classic dish.

2 tbl peanut oil
3 slices smoked bacon, chopped
½ cup (2 ½ oz/60 g) red onion, finely chopped
1 clove garlic, finely diced
2 ribs celery, finely diced
1 small yellow bell pepper, de-seeded, de-veined and finely diced
1 green bell pepper, de-seeded, de-veined and finely diced

1 tsp thyme
1 tsp garlic salt
1 cup (8 fl oz/250 ml) V-8 juice
3 ½ cups (1 lb 2 ½ oz/510 g) peeled plum tomatoes, mashed with your hands
2 cups (10 oz/250 g) long-grain rice – cooked in chicken stock

Heat the oil and saute the bacon, onion, garlic, celery and bell peppers for 5 minutes.

Add all the seasoning and the V-8 juice and the tomatoes. Cook for 3 minutes, stirring well. Remove from the heat and mix in the rice. Portion into, ideally, 2 oz/45 g ramekins. Re-heat when needed.

Sauteed Crawfish

If you cannot find any mudbugs (aka crawfish or crayfish) use smaller fresh shrimp.

2 tbl unsalted butter

3 scallion stalks, chopped

1 cup (5 oz/125 g) crawfish

1 tbl white wine

1 tsp soy sauce

1 tbl Kenny's Seafood Seasoning (see p. 21)

Melt the butter and add the scallions for 2 minutes. Add the rest of the ingredients and cook for 5 minutes. Keep warm.

Old-fashioned Tomato Sauce

This is how tomato sauce should be made. Tomato sauce has to be fresh. You will need to search out a proper, ripe and flavorful tomato. (Please forget tinned tomatoes; I know this is not easy, but it's definitely worth the effort.)

4 1/2 cups (1 1/2 lb/635 g) tomatoes, quartered

1/2 cup (4 fl oz/125 ml) olive oil

1/2 small onion, diced

Puree the tomatoes and strain. Discard the juice. Heat the oil over a medium heat. Add the onion and saute until soft – about 5 minutes. Add the strained tomatoes and bring to a boil. Reduce the heat and cook for a further 10 minutes. Use immediately.

Place your rice ramekins on the plates. Surround with the tomato sauce and surround the sauce with the crawfish. Garnish with snipped chives and serve.

If you fancy cooking a seafood version, why not use Seafood Dirty Rice (see p. 118), in place of my regular Jambalaya rice?

Seafood Dirty Rice

1 rib celery, finely diced

1 green bell pepper, cored and diced

1 red onion, finely diced

2 tbl unsalted butter

1 tsp sea salt

1 clove garlic, finely diced

1 tsp cayenne pepper

$^1/_2$ tsp ground black pepper

$^1/_2$ tsp ground white pepper

$^1/_2$ tsp thyme

1 tbl paprika

5 cups (2 pints/1.2 litres) fish stock

3 cups (1 lb/450 g) rice

$^1/_2$ cup (2 $^1/_2$ oz/60 g) crushed plum
tomatoes, with a tsp tomato puree

5 shrimp per serving

3 cups (1 lb/450 g) fish cuttings, no bones

chopped scallions, for garnish

Saute the vegetables in the butter for 5 minutes. Add the seasonings and mix well. Bring the stock to a boil and add the rice. Cook for 8 minutes, then remove from the heat. Stir in the tomato mix. Cover and allow to steam for 10 minutes.

Add the shrimp and fish, then return to the heat for 10 minutes. Keep stirring. Strain and then portion. Top with the scallions.

This recipe can be really serious. I'm giving you an easy version. If you want the extensive one drop me a line. My e-mail address is at the back of the book.

Fried Chicken

Fried chicken is the best meal on our planet. Fattening it is, but when fat is a building block for sex hormones, why should we care?

Originally I thought the Hummingbird in New Orleans was the only place to eat fried chicken, but I have since discovered Gus's Fried Chicken, Highway 70, Mason, 40 miles outside Memphis, Tennessee. A yellow sign highlighting a black chicken surrounded by a garish blinking neon heralds your arrival at this temple for the finest of fried chicken. Gus will not share his recipe – here is my attempt. Use peanut oil for frying. It is best to fry in a cast-iron skillet, but your heaviest pan will work.

a 3 lb/1.3 kg bird – the best you can find,
never frozen, cut into tenths
1 tbl jalapeño Tabasco – the green one
1 tbl snipped chives
milk
2 cups (10 oz/250 g) all-purpose flour

2 tsp garlic salt
2 tsp ground white pepper
1 tsp paprika
1 tsp sugar
1 tsp thyme
peanut oil

Place the chicken in a bowl, pour over the jalapeño Tabasco and sprinkle with the chives. Cover the bird with milk. Refrigerate for at least 1 hour.

Combine all the dry ingredients and mix well. Heat enough oil to semi submerge the chicken pieces to the point where it slightly spits when you drop some beer in it. Pre-heat the oven to 350°F/180°C/gas mark 4.

Using your left hand drop the chicken pieces, one at a time, into the flour. With your right hand toss until the chicken is covered. Repeat. Just remember to keep one hand for wet and one for dry otherwise you'll get a sticky paw and that's sloppy. Once all the chicken pieces are coated carefully drop them in the oil. Do not overcrowd the skillet, cook in batches if you cannot get them all in. Carefully turn the pieces a few times until they begin to turn brown. When they stop 'popping' – about 25 minutes – transfer to a paper towel to drain, then place in the oven for 10 minutes to finish cooking and to ensure real juiciness.

Test the chicken is fully cooked before you serve up. Then eat the biggest piece yourself, because you made it and therefore deserve it. This dish is so good your guests will be bugging you to hold another party real soon, I promise.

Mashed Potatoes

Mashed potatoes are a good vehicle for playing with a myriad of flavors. Chile and garlic served with cheese is my favorite.

Boil your potatoes until the skin begins to peel off. Quickly drain and run under cold water for 1 minute. Transfer to a mixing bowl and drop in butter, chives, garlic salt and double cream. Mash. I like to keep the skins on – you may not.

Now add your chile and garlic or your creamed horseradish if you like. Once your primary ingredients are mixed in, add some chopped scallions, coarse-ground black pepper and soy sauce. Serve warm. If you fancy the cheese idea, simply top with a sharp Cheddar and broil until the cheese is nearly burnt.

Turnip or Mustard Greens

Greens are a Southern favorite. It the leaves of a root vegetable, the bit most people disgard.

4 bunches greens, about 4 lb/1.8 kg
1/2 cup (2 1/2 oz/60 g) bacon drippings or lard
8 oz/185 g smoked ham
1 onion, diced
1 rib celery, finely diced
2 cloves garlic, finely diced
1 tbl parsley, finely chopped

1/2 tsp thyme
pinch of celery salt
pinch of ground white pepper
1/2 tsp cayenne
1 cup (8 fl oz/250 ml) water
1 tsp sugar
a dash of white wine vinegar

Wash the greens and pick off the leaves. Soak well in fresh water before use. Heat the lard and add the ham, onion, celery, garlic and parsley. Saute for 10 minutes. Add the seasonings and cook for a further 10 minutes.

Add the water and bring to a boil, add the sugar and vinegar. As soon as bubbles start forming add the greens. Stir well. Take off the heat and cover for at least 10 minutes before use.

Pot Likker

Pot likker is essentially the liquid result of cooking greens. Sometimes folk make it into a meal in itself. If you do, try it with Dog Biscuits – cornmeal batter fried in bacon fat.

Pot likker has a strange resonance for anyone unaccustomed to Southern ways. This does not surprise me. Have you read *The Ballad Of the Sad Cafe* by Carson McCullers? Here's a snippet: 'Each night the hunchback came down the stairs with the air of one who has a grand opinion of himself. He always smelled slightly of turnip greens, as Miss Amelia rubbed him night and morning with pot liquor to give him strength.' There you go!

½ cup (2 oz/45 g) diced ham hock meat	*1 ½ tsp salt*
½ cup (2 ½ oz/60 g) white onion, chopped	*½ tsp cayenne pepper*
4 tbl bacon fat	*6 cups (2 lb/900 g) greens – turnip, mustard,*
1 tsp sugar	*kale, collards or good old spinach – cleaned*
7 cups (2 pints 16 fl oz/1.75 litres) water	*and stemmed*

Over a moderate heat saute the ham and onion in the bacon fat, until the onion is soft. Remove from the heat and mix in the sugar. Set aside.

Bring the water and seasonings to boil. Cook for 20 minutes Add the greens, put the lid on the pot and cook for another 20 minutes. Mix in the onion and ham. Allow to cool for 20 minutes. The pot likker is the juice, but you may want to serve the whole lot.

To garnish the southern way, add pepper sauce and Indian dumplings. Pepper sauce is made by steeping green cayenne peppers in cider vinegar and the dumplings are gnocchi-like cornmeal dumplings.

White Gravy

You want to learn southern cookin'? Then this is the recipe you have to master. You'll need to have roasted a chicken first. And remember to serve the gravy on the side, not over your entree.

2 tbl fat and drippings from the chicken roasting pan
½ cup (2 ½ oz/60 g) unsmoked ham, julienned

1 small white onion, finely diced
2 tbl all-purpose flour, seasoned with salt and pepper
2 cups (16 fl oz/500 ml) buttermilk

Strain the fat into a skillet. Over a medium heat stir in the ham and onion and cook for 3 minutes. Add the flour and stir constantly. Without burning, turn the flour brown. Gradually add the buttermilk – keep stirring. Bring to a low boil. Cook for 5 minutes.

If there's too much, then save the gravy for a midnite snack, serving it over white rice. Beats cold potato salad.

Spinach Cornbread

My favorite Elvis song, albeit written by Tony Joe White, is 'Poke Salad Annie'. In Blanchard, Louisiana, close to where Tony is from, they celebrate this wild green every May. Its stalks and berries are poisonous and the leaves must be boiled twice to be edible. Yet some folk will steal it out of your gunny sack to savor its spinach-like flavor. To be less adventurous, here's a spinach cornbread recipe for sopping up your white gravy.

½ cup (2 ½ oz/60 g) sifted all-purpose flour
1 ½ cups (7 ½ oz/185 g) cornmeal – if you
are in the States I mean yellow cornmeal
1 tsp salt
2 tsp sugar
3 tsp baking powder

3 eggs, lightly beaten
1 cup (8 fl oz/250 ml) milk
3 cups (1 lb/450 g) steamed spinach
¼ cup (2 ½ fl oz/60 ml) double cream
½ cup (2 ½ oz/60 g) unsalted butter, melted

Pre-heat the oven to 425°F/220°C/gas mark 7.

Sift, as always, the dry ingredients together into a bowl.

In your favorite bowl, blend together the flour-cornmeal mix with the eggs and milk. Add the spinach, cream and butter. Beat lightly, then transfer to your oiled and pre-heated cornbread baking skillet. (This ensures a golden crust and should eliminate any sticking.)

Bake for about 20 minutes, depending on the size of your skillet, or when a toothpick comes out clean

Barbecue

Barbecuing is huge in the States. Two towns vie for the right to be called the Barbecue Capital – Memphis and Kansas City. I have decided to go with Memphis as my favorite, despite the presence of the venerable Arthur Bryant's in Kansas. Aesthetically, Bryant's resembles a men's room. But the restaurant serves wonderful ribs, in a uniquely grainy sauce. In Kansas City beef brisket and spare ribs are the main specialities, all cooked in a vinegar-tomato sauce

In Memphis the range and history of barbecue cooking is awesome. Memphis barbecue originated with the slaves. After preparing food for their owners they would cook the leftover parts for themselves in outdoor barbecue pits. The Memphis Yellow Pages lists 32 barbecue restaurants and 86 barbecue joints. My favorite Memphis soulfood restaurants are Cozy Corner at 745 North Parkway and Jim Neely's Interstate Bar-B-Que, both serving some of the finest barbecue you are ever likely to find. Note – most Memphis barbecue joints don't serve booze, which can be rather disheartening to say the least.

In Memphis, pork shoulder and ribs are the mainstay, cooked very slowly with a dry rub.

My rubs for cooking Memphis barbecue are in the pantry section. Cooking the meats real slow is not too difficult to work out.

Before we leave barbecue I have to mention the Bahama Village in Key West. Key West offers a solid base of local seafoods with Cuban and Bahamian influences (Cuba is only 90 miles away). On weekends, the Bahama Village, just off Duval Street – the main drag – is the place in town for barbecue. The barbecues are set right on the street and often give the money they make to the church or other non-profit organizations. My favorite snack was a short slab of pork ribs on white bread. The single paper towel given to you is not enough. Finish the messy sandwich and head to the Green Parrot for a cold Heineken. There is very little to touch the whole experience.

Jerked Fried Chicken with Mango– Habanero Chutney and Spiced Pumpkin Muffins

A lack of jerk and a lack of gospel in my life prompted me to invent this dish. Yvonne Lola Bell – owner of Lola's at 30 W. 22nd St, between 5th and 6th Avenues in New York City – introduced me to gospel brunch. Lola's is my only 'must stop' when I'm in town.

Serve the chicken on a bed of lettuce. Side the chutney and the muffins and provide plenty of cold beer – this is a spicy meal.

a 3 lb/1.3 kg chicken, cut into tenths

For the jerk sauce
2 tbl olive oil
4 cloves garlic, diced
4 cups (1 1/4 lb/500 g) white onions, quartered
1 1/2 cups (8 oz/185 g) habañeros, de-seeded, de-veined and quartered

2/3 cup (4 oz/100 g) fresh ginger, peeled
1/4 cup (1 1/4 oz/30 g) allspice
3 tbl fresh thyme
3 tbl coarse-ground black pepper
1 cup (8 fl oz/250 ml) cider vinegar
1 cup (8 fl oz/250 ml) soy sauce
1/4 cup (2 1/2 fl oz/60 ml) dark rum
2 tbl fresh lime juice

Pulse the oil, garlic, onions, chiles and ginger in your food processor until smooth. Transfer to a mixing bowl. Add the rest of the ingredients and thoroughly mix. Coat the chicken with the jerk sauce. Cover and refrigerate for 24 hours.

Pre-heat the oven to 350°F/180°C/gas mark 4. Transfer the chicken to a roasting pan and bake for 45 minutes or so. Keep basting. Remove from the oven. Make sure the bird is thoroughly covered in the sauce and then place under the broiler to seal properly.

Mango-Habanero Chutney

2 tbl olive oil
1 tbl white onion, finely diced
1 clove garlic, finely diced
½ tsp grated ginger
2 red jalapeños, de-seeded, de-veined and finely chopped
1 habañero, de-seeded, de-veined and finely chopped

½ cup (2 ½ oz/60 g) sugar
¾ tsp oregano
½ tsp ground cinnamon
½ tsp salt
1 cup (8 fl oz/250 ml) cider vinegar
2 cups (10 oz/250 g) mango flesh

Heat the oil and saute the onion, garlic and ginger until the onion is soft. Add the chiles, sugar, oregano, cinnamon and salt and cook for 10 more minutes – keep stirring. With a slotted spoon remove the ingredients. De-glaze the pan with vinegar until it's thick then add the mango. Cook for 2 minutes then remove from the heat.

Allow to cool. Transfer to a jar and seal. Chill for 24 hours before use.

Spiced Pumpkin Muffins

1 ¼ cups (6 ¼ oz/155 g) all-purpose flour
3 tsp baking powder
¼ tsp salt
½ tsp ground cinnamon
½ tsp cayenne
¼ tsp nutmeg
½ cup (2 ½ oz/60 g) lard
¾ cup (3 ¾ oz/90 g) brown sugar

2 large eggs
1 cup (5 oz/125 g) pumpkin flesh, diced small
½ cup (4 fl oz/125 ml) milk
¼ cup (1 ¼ oz/30 g) raisins
2 tbl white sugar
½ tsp ground cinnamon

Pre-heat the oven to 375°F/190°C/gas mark 5. In a mixing bowl sift together the dry ingredients. Cream the lard and brown sugar together until fluffy. Beat the eggs then mix into the lard. Beat in the pumpkin and mix well. Add the dry ingredients and gently mix in. Then gently mix in the milk and raisins until the milk is thoroughly incorporated.

With softened butter, grease a 12-muffin tin. Combine the white sugar and cinnamon ready for dusting. Spoon the batter into the muffin cups, about ²/₃ full. Sprinkle the sugar-cinnamon mix over the top. Bake for about 20 minutes or until a toothpick comes out clean. Let cool for 5 minutes before turning out.

Red Snapper Ceviche Salad with Blackeyed Pea Salsa

Ceviche (prononouced 'se-vee-chay') originated somewhere in Latin America (Peru gets most folk's vote). Initially it developed as a way of preserving food before refrigeration. The acidity of the lime juice effectively cooks and preserves the fish. Any seafood will probably work (except the oily dark meats, such as mackerel) if you ensure the product is top quality and extremely fresh. If you manage to acquire cool seafood this recipe is a treat.

1 red jalapeño, de-seeded, de-veined and finely chopped
4 6 oz/150 g red snapper fillets, chopped into 1-inch squares
1 red onion, finely diced
¹/₃ cup (3 fl oz/75 ml) orange juice

¹/₂ cup (2 ¹/₂ oz/60 g) sweet potato, peeled, cubed and boiled
¹/₂ cup (2 ¹/₂ oz/60 g) cilantro leaves, chopped
1 tsp olive oil
¹/₂ cup (2 ¹/₂ oz/60 g) corn kernels, roasted
¹/₂ cup (4 fl oz/125 ml) fresh lime juice

Combine all ingredients and chill for 12 hours. Shred a little lettuce and spread over your serving plates. Centre the salsa and spread the ceviche around the salsa. Keep the presentation simple.

Blackeyed Pea Salsa

The blackeyed pea, also known as the cow pea, is one of the world's greatest vegeatables. It has a distinctive, earthy flavor. Cook until soft and mix it with an equal amount of Salsa Fresca (see p. 15). Traditionally blackeyed peas are eaten on New Year's Eve for good luck.

Chilaquiles

This is my own take on the traditional New Mexican dish using leftovers. Chilaquiles translates as 'broken-up sombrero', which refers to dry corn tortilla strips, that can be used any way you like. Visually this is my favorite dish – it looks like a Mexican lasagne. But it does require a decent-sized broiler or an extremely hot oven.

For the 'lasagne' mix
2 tbl olive oil
2 medium zucchinis, thinly sliced
1 cup (5 oz/125 g) button mushrooms, thinly sliced
1 small green bell pepper, cored and diced
1 small yellow bell pepper, cored and diced
1 red jalapeño, de-seeded, de-veined and finely diced
1 small red onion, finely chopped
2 scallion stalks, finely chopped
2 tbl My General Seasoning (see p. 23)
1/2 cup (4 fl oz/125 ml) white wine

3 6-inch tortillas per person, cut into squares and fried or broiled until crisp
1 1/2 cups (8 oz/185 g) Monterey Jack cheese, grated
1 cup (8 fl oz/250 ml) Salsa Verde (see p. 15)
1/2 cup (4 fl oz/125 ml) tamarillo juice – simply peel the fruit and press through a strainer
1/2 cup (2 1/2 oz/60 g) cilantro leaves, chopped

Over a high heat saute the oil and all the vegetables for 3 minutes. Add the seasoning and cook for a further 4 minutes. Add the wine until it has nearly evaporated. Remember to keep stirring. Reserve and keep warm.

Pre-heat the oven to 425°F/220°C/gas mark 7.

For each serving take a tortilla square and smother with a little of the veg. mix. Top with cheese. Repeat with another. Then top each stack with a third square. Top each 'lasagne' with cheese. Place under the broiler and cook until the cheese is slightly brown. Place each stack on a baking tray and bake for 10 minutes.

Spread the salsa around each plate and dot with the tamarillo juice. Centre a stack of chilaquiles and serve decorated with cilantro.

Buffalo Pot Pie

The best Chicken Pot Pie is found at The Cafe in Manhattan's Grand Central Station. The term 'pot pie' first appeared in 1792 and refers to a deep pot lined with pastry and stuffed with meat and vegetables. Following the current trend for strange meats like ostrich, alligator, wild boar, antelope and bear, I have decided to offer you a buffalo pot pie.

The population of buffalo in the States used to number in excess of 60 million. However, by the late 19th century the number was below one thousand. The primary reason for this push to extinction was the white settlers' determination to kill off the Native American Indians – buffalo was their primary meat source. Thankfully President Roosevelt saved the animal by establishing reservations in 1905. If you don't live on the wide-open prairie try venison as a substitute.

3 cups (1 lb/450 g) bison chuck steak, cubed
2 tbl peanut oil
1 tbl all-purpose flour

For the stock
5 cups (2 pints/1.2 litres) beef stock

2 white onions, coarsely chopped
1 carrot, finely diced
2 ribs celery, diced
1 cup (5 oz/125 g) green peas
1 tbl white roux
1 tbl My General Seasoning (see p. 23)

Toss the steak in half the oil, then dredge in the flour. Heat the remaining oil and brown the steak.

Bring the stock ingredients to the boil. Lower to a simmer and pop in the meat. Cook for 60 minutes. Allow to cool.

You now need a pastry-lined pot, with a pastry cover (store-bought short crust is fine), chilled and ready. You know how to do this. Right? Brush the top with an egg yolk wash.

Fill the pot with the mix, place on the lid and bake for 90 minutes, or until the top is browned. I could walk you through the process, but that would be dull.

Pizza

Pizza has no definite history to speak of, other than the fact that it probably originated in Italy. But it resembles too many other culinary ideas to be pigeonholed too easily. The analogies with Middle Eastern bread seem credible, given their similar texture and taste, but who knows?

In my opinion the best pizza is the simplest pizza – such as you will find at Ruby's at 489 Third Street in San Francisco. Under the sign of the big tomato, a thick cornmeal-crusted pizza with a molten sea of tomatoes and five cheeses is served – no pineapple, smoked kangaroo or pickled crickets for me either, thanks.

For the dough
1 cup (8 fl oz/250 ml) warm water
1 tsp sugar
1 pack active dried yeast
3 1/4 cups (1lb 1 1/4 oz/480 g) all-purpose flour
1/2 tsp salt
1 tsp thyme
3 tbl olive oil
cayenne
oregano
garlic salt

Pour the water into a medium-sized bowl. Add the sugar and yeast and mix with a fork until frothy. Allow to sit in a warm place for 25 minutes.

Sift the flour, salt and thyme together. Add to the yeast and mix again with a wooden spoon. After the dough starts to pull away from the sides add 2 tbsp of the oil and knead with floured hands for 5 minutes. Form the dough into a ball and rub all over with oil. Cover with oiled cling film. Allow to rise to twice its size. This should take about an hour, depending on how good your yeast has worked. Knead again – punching out the air – and allow to rise again for another hour.

Pre-heat the oven to 500°F/250°C/gas mark 10 or as hot as it will go. Then roll the dough into two 46cm (18 in) pies. Rub with oil and sprinkle with cayenne, oregano and garlic salt. Now it's time to add your topping. I suggest the following, although I know you will add your favorites, just don't be too zany.

The basic topping is a combination of tomatoes, peeled and cored, and seasoned tomato puree (this is puree seasoned with Pepper Seasoning (see p. 24)). Then top with fresh shrimp, diced; boiled pulled pork; steamed spinach and eggs; 5 types of diced onion – garlic, white onion, chives, scallions and leeks. Then smother in Italian mozzarella and slowly bake.

Toasted fresh herbs are often present on my pizzas. Toasting seems to intensify the flavors and removes any aftertaste. Oregano and rosemary are my favorites.

Baking tiles are the best for even cooking. If you don't have any, use a baking sheet. The baking should take 20–25 minutes or until the crust is golden in color.

Native American Cooking

It is not my place to inform you about the history of the folk who first inhabitated North America. But I strongly suggest you check out the facts. Not a pretty story. And as the Zuni Chiefs, Palowathtiwa, Waihusiwa and Heluta, said in 1886: 'Strange people, strange people these Americans.'

The diet of the native Indian before the European intrusion was fairly rudimentary, but interesting nevertheless. As one would expect from a large continent there is a huge variety. Here are a few of my favorites which I first presented at an alternative Thanksgiving dinner. I feel the Choctaws of Louisiana, the Mohegans of New York and the Blackfoots of the Rockies, along with all other tribes, deserve to be in any book celebrating the food of North America.

Blackfoot Gut with Mushroom Gravy

This is a beef sausage made by the Blackfoot tribe of the northern plains. As with haggis, guts or intenstines are traditionally used as a casing.

Mince together 2 cups (10 oz/250 g) bison, elk or any beef tenderloin with ¼ cup (1 ¼ oz/30 g) lard. Finely chop up 3 cups (1 lb/450 g) mixed fresh veggies, such as carrots, onions, potatoes and squash and then combine with the meat. Add some herbs (traditionally sage, thyme and cattail pollen) and a little flour, then stuff your casings. If you can't buy sausage casings simply form into patties.

Mushroom Gravy

Gravies are best made from the drippings left in roasting pans – regardless of what you roasted. Into the drippings you whisk flour and then some sauteed vegetables. If you haven't recently been roasting, use a stock.

For my Mushroom Gravy, I roast carrots, celery and onion, dice them and then add to the drippings. I double the volume with red wine and bring to a simmer. This I allow to cook for 10 minutes. I then add re-hydrated wild mushrooms, usually ceps, and cook for 10 minutes. I strain the mix and then add a little seasoning, some diced mushrooms and a little butter. Mix well and keep the gravy warm.

Pawnee Roast Guinea Fowl with Re-fried Pinto Beans and Zuni Succotash

This recipe from Nebraska is, thanks to the honey, sweet potatoes and guinea fowl, a buttery delight. The Pawnees, who were farmers, migrated from East Texas in the 13th century to what is now known as the state of Nebraska, hence the south-western accompaniments. The guinea fowl is my preference over the indigenous turkey – the traditional bird for this recipe.

As it's cooking brush the bird with honey. Also add to the baking tray parboiled sweet potatoes. When the bird is nearly cooked (an average-sized guinea fowl will take about 50 minutes), stuff the potatoes inside it. Turn the heat off, but leave the bird in the oven for a further 30 minutes. At home I serve a whole guinea fowl to my guests. You may prefer to cut the bird in half. Surround the plate with your succotash, centre the bird and top with the beans. Leave under the broiler for 3 minutes before serving.

Re-fried Pinto Beans

A staple of the Mexican peasant diet and one of the world's finest comfort foods.

Take some cooked beans, add some bacon drippings, finely chopped onion and some seasoning. Heat for 20 minutes. Some people mash them, others eat them whole. It's up to you.

Zuni Succotash

Follow the basic idea of my Ham Succotash on p. 114 but use venison, onion, tomatoes, corn, green beans and crushed sunflower seeds instead. The Zuni are a tribe from the Rio Grande in the south-west.

Medicine Sausage

This is a real winner. If you make your own sausages you are in for a treat. If you don't, then make patties out of the mix. Traditionally it is made by the Cheyenne tribe from the Plains from the flesh of a virile young bison bull. In a time-honoured rite of passage at the Sun Dance, young men would take a bite of the sausage and declare the name of the girl they wished to marry.

The recipe is simple. Season ground bison or venison with salt and pepper. Stuff in casings, tie and roast in a pre-heated oven at 375°F/190°C/gas mark 5 for 15 minutes. Place 6 oz/150 g fresh sage on a sheet of tin foil. Place the sausages on top and wrap tightly. Let the sausages cool in the sage for 90 minutes.

Maybe serve on their own for a brunch appetizer.

Choctaw Leather Britches Bean Stew

This recipe came originally from a Louisiana tribe. Britches Bean Stew is a colourful version of a winter dish featuring green beans and salt pork. The term Leather Britches comes from the way young green beans look as they are hung out to dry. Green back bacon is an unsmoked, briefly cured cut from the loin along a pig's back.

I like to serve this as a side order, but you may wish to make the Britches a centerpiece. If you do you will need a bread for sopping up. The Algonquin Hoe Cake would be ideal. This is an unleavened cornbread, seasoned with dill. But I'll leave it up to you.

5 cups (2 pints/1.2 litres) chicken stock
1 tsp sea salt
1 tsp coarse-ground black pepper
pinch of thyme
pinch of oregano

2/3 cup (4 oz/100 g) green back bacon, de-rinded and diced
3 cups (1 lb/450 g) green beans
1 tbl cornflour
1/4 cup (2 1/2 fl oz/60 ml) water

Bring the stock to boil with the seasonings. Fry the bacon until it is crisp. Add to the stock. After 10 minutes add the beans and cook until tender. With a slotted spoon remove the beans. Mix the cornflour with the water and add to the stock. Whisk in well. Remove from the heat and replace the beans. Let this rest for 10 minutes and serve.

Gefilte Fish

I have previously documented the strong influence of Jewish folk on American culinary culture. By the 1880s thousands of Yiddish-speaking Jews had fled from Russia, Poland, Hungary etc., and settled on the Lower East Side of Manhatten. Gefilte fish, boiled beef, herring with horseradish and strudels arrived with them.

Gefilte is a German term for 'stuffed'. It is a freshwater fish loaf or dumplings, seasoned with chopped eggs, onions and pepper, and cooked in fresh fish stock. This is my favorite Jewish recipe.

A mix of three fish works best, such as pike, grayling, carp or chub.

2 slices white bread, crusts removed
4 cups (1 ½ lb/600 g) ground freshwater fish
1 large onion, grated
1 large onion, sliced
2 eggs
3 white fish bones, with heads

1 tsp sea salt
1 tsp coarse-ground black pepper
saffron (optional)
horseradish, dill pickles and julienned carrots for serving

Soak the bread in cold water. Combine the fish, onion and eggs. Drain the bread and mix in with the fish. Pulse the mix in your blender for about 20 minutes. We want the mix fluffy and sticky which will result in light dumplings.

Put the fish bones in a pot and cover with water. Add the salt and pepper.

Shape the fish mixture into 3 x 2 inch egg shapes. Place the dozen or so gefilte fish in the pot and bring to boil. Reduce the heat and partially cover. Cook for two hours. (You may wish to dissolve some saffron in the water – as the end-product may have an unappetizingly gray appearance.) Remove the pot from the heat and allow to sit for 10 minutes. Transfer the gefilte fish to a casscrole dish. Strain the liquid and pour over the fish. Chill until the liquid has gelled. Serve cold, with buckets of horseradish, dill pickles and julienned carrots.

Soulfood

More than just a list of dishes, soulfood is the name given to a certain attitude to food held by poor black and white folk from the south. It involves richly flavored ingredients and simply prepared foods, but more than anything it's an attitude. Like the Blues it's hard to pin down but goes a lot further than what you see at first. It's down home, stick-to-your-ribs, happy food that you cook and eat by all the senses. Food to enjoy with friends. A recipe book for soulfood is really quite useless, it's all down to the intuitive feel and respect you have for your food. Enjoy these recipes.

Creamed Corn

Serve with your fried chicken.

1 tbl bacon fat or lard
6 ears corn, roasted and the kernels cut off
2 tbl all-purpose flour
2 tbl sugar

1/2 cup (4 fl oz/125 ml) single cream
1 tsp My General Seasoning (see p. 23)
1/2 cup (4 fl oz/125 ml) milk

We are after a soupy mix. Heat the bacon fat (for some weird reason American bacon produces a decent amount of fat after broiling; British bacon does not). As soon as it can spit add the corn. Cook for 3 minutes.

Sift the flour and sugar into the cream, and mix into the corn. Add the seasoning and the milk. Whisk well, then simmer until the sauce is thickish.

Coleslaw

I hate this recipe, but most folk love it. Someone help them; or at least teach them a quality dance. A must at all barbecues and picnics.

1/2 small head white cabbage, shredded
1/2 small head red cabbage, shredded
1 small white onion, grated
1 cup (5 oz/125 g) carrots, grated
1 cup (8 fl oz/250 ml) mayonnaise
1/2 cup (2 1/2 oz/60 g) sugar

1 cup (8 fl oz/250 ml) sour cream
1 tbl white wine vinegar
1 tsp sea salt
1 tsp coarse-ground black pepper
1 tsp celery seeds

The recipe is a hit or miss affair. Feel free to experiment, adding new or subtracting existing ingredients. Mix all the ingredients together and refrigerate.

Candied Yams

Why always potatoes? Candied yams make a great foil for any roast dish.

4 cups (1 1/2 lb/600 g) sweet potatoes, peeled, parboiled and mashed
1 cup (5 oz/125 g) brown sugar
1/4 cup (2 1/2 fl oz/60 ml) orange juice

3 tbl butter
1 tsp vanilla extract
1/2 tsp grated nutmeg

Pre-heat the oven to 325°F/170°C/gas mark 3.

Mix the ingredients well. Transfer to your favorite casserole dish. Maybe butter it first. Place in the oven for 20 minutes. Allow the candied yams to cool a little. Keep warm.

Pig's Feet

If you were to travel back in time to a New Year's Eve dinner at a North Carolina plantation you would find the black folk serving a glorious feast. Along with Hoppin' John (blackeyed peas and rice) you'd, for certain, find Pig's Feet on the menu.

12 pigs' feet, halved and cleaned
4 cups (1 3/4 pints/1 litre) cider vinegar
4 ribs celery, coarsely chopped
4 large onions, coarsely chopped
4 carrots, coarsely chopped

4 bay leaves
1 tbl peppercorns
1 tbl cayenne pepper
2 tbl salt

Place all ingredients in a large pot and cover with cold water. Bring to the boil, then reduce heat, cover and simmer for 3 hours. The feet are ready when the meat is fork tender. Please do not allow to stick. This is all you need to know. Just eat.

Spoonbread

This bread is so called because you should be able to spoon it on to your plate. Others say it gets its name from an Indian word for porridge – suppawn. It's the perfect accompaniment for any sauce or stew.

1 cup (5 oz/125 g) cornmeal
1 tsp salt
1 tsp baking powder
2 cups (16 fl oz/250 ml) water

1 cup (8 fl oz/125 ml) buttermilk
2 tbl butter, melted
3 egg yolks, beaten
3 egg whites, stiffly beaten

Pre-heat the oven to 375°F/190°C/gas mark 5.

Sift the dry ingredients together. Fold in the rest of the ingredients. Lightly mix. Pour into a small loaf tin and bake for 15 minutes. Allow to cool a little, then serve. Remember it's Spoonbread.

Smothered Pork Chops

Skid row was initially a term that referred to a road built by loggers to skid fallen trees down to the water. Eventually it was used to denote a part of town where loggers, sailors, Indians and other hard-working, party dudes hung out. One legendary Portland skid row saloon built in the early 1800s was Erickson's. It occupied an entire block, had five entrances, a 684-foot linear bar and offered free lunches. One item on the menu was half a roast ox. I guess they portioned it.

This is what I would serve as 'free lunch' in my Skid Row saloon.

6 8 oz/185 g pork chops, trimmed of the rind
but not the fat.
1 tbl Pepper Seasoning (see p. 24)
1 cup (5 oz/125 g) all-purpose flour
2 tbl unsalted butter
3 cups (1 ¼ pints/700 ml) chicken stock

1 tbl Worcestershire sauce
2 cups (10 oz/250 g) mushrooms, chopped
1 onion, finely chopped
1 tsp thyme
½ cup (4 fl oz/125 ml) white wine
1 tbl parsley, finely chopped

Dust the chops in the seasoning and flour. Melt the butter and evenly brown the chops.

Heat the stock and add the rest of the ingredients. Cook for 20 minutes. Drop in the chops, lower the heat and cook for 60 minutes. Cover if you wish. Serve with fluffy white rice.

Lobster Newburg

This dish is a rich blend of lobster and a shellfish cream sauce. Its was invented in 1876 by a publicist for Delmonico's restaurant in New York. The kitchens of the Delmonico brothers apparently invented many culinary dishes, although I don't think Baked Alaska is one I'd be too proud of – my mother, and probably yours, would disagree.

2 large live lobsters – around 2 lb/900 g each
⅔ cup (4 oz/100 g) unsalted butter
2 tsp sea salt
¼ tsp grated nutmeg
¼ tsp white pepper

¼ tsp cayenne
1 cup (8 fl oz/250 ml) double cream
4 egg yolks
1 tbl brandy
paprika for dusting

Boil the lobsters in salted water for 10-12 minutes. You want them undercooked at this stage as they will continue cooking in the sauce. Pull off the claws and cut off the heads. Discard the heads. Split the tail shells in half and remove the meat. Wash the empty tail shells and save. Cut the tail meat into large chunks. Split the claws and chop the meat in a similar fashion.

Melt the butter with seasonings. Add all the lobster and simmer for 2 minutes. Mix the cream, egg yolks and brandy. Pour the mix into the lobster pan and stir until the sauce begins to thicken. Spoon the mixture into the empty shells, sprinkle with paprika and place under your broiler – at a moderate heat – until the top begins to brown.

Crab works well with this recipe too, but serve it in the crab shells.

One outrageous restaurant where you can eat lobster, in a multitude of presentations, is the Two Lights Lobster Shack off Route 77 in Maine. A classic seafood restaurant, only open between late April and early October, it is in a captivating, rocky setting just south of Portland. They serve lobster rolls, lobster stews, plain lobsters, clams, fish and just about anything else they can catch. Well worth a visit.

Tamales

A tamale consists of ground cornmeal (*masa harina*) dough stuffed with a suitable filling (traditionally seasoned meat), wrappped in a corn husk and steamed. It may sound a little odd, but enclosing a meal in a husk is as old as the Aztecs. So don't knock it. Otherwise Netty, of Netty's on Silverlake Blvd in LA. who serves the best tamales, despite the prison like chain-link fence around the joint, might come over and teach you the meaning of the word respect.

Tamales can be stuffed with anything. Similarly they can be
served with anything. Try any one or a combination of black bean,
red chile and tomatillo sauces.

For the dough
4 cups (1 ¹/₂ lb/600 g) masa harina
¹/₃ cup (2 oz/45 g) all-purpose flour
2 tbl My Chili Seasoning (see p. 25)
¹/₂ tsp garlic salt
¹/₂ tsp garlic powder
¹/₂ tsp baking powder (this is not authentic,
but I feel it helps make lighter tamales)
1 tbl chives, snipped

1 ³/₄ cups (14 fl oz/425 ml) warm water
2 tbl olive oil

1 cup (5 oz/125 g) crawfish tails
¹/₂ cup (2 ¹/₂ oz/60 g) scallions, chopped
1 tsp oyster sauce
1 tbl Kenny's Seafood Seasoning (see p. 21)
dried corn husks

Sift together the masa, flour, chili seasoning, garlic salt, garlic powder and baking powder.
Mix in the chives. Transfer to your mixer. With the motor running, slowly add the water and
oil. The dough needs to be firm, yet a little elastic and moist. Above all it needs to be easily
handled. Form the dough into about 20 thick oblong shapes, 6 inches long.

Meanwhile, in your blender pulse the crawfish, scallions, oyster sauce and seafood
seasoning until the mix is coarsely chopped.

Slightly flatten each dough ball. Spread a tablespoon of the crawfish mix in the centre.
Push the sides of the dough over the mix. We want the mix covered.

Soak your corn husks in water for 1 hour (obviously there should be as many husks as
dough balls). Peel off two thin strips of husk from the edges of each. Place a filled dough
ball in the middle of each husk. Wrap the husk around the dough and tie at each end with
the strips of husk, alternatively use a piece of string.

Prepare a steamer. Chinese steamers are efficient, but a colander over a pot of water
works just as well. Steam the tamales over boiling water for roughly 15 minutes or until the
masa is cooked. Untie one end and open the tamale. Serve two to a portion and surround
with your chosen sauce.

BIG SALADS

Caesar Salad

The Caesar salad was created by Caesar Cardini, an Italian immigrant and restaurateur in the Mexican border town of Tijuana, in 1924. Cardini's salad is everywhere and often an embarrassment. This is not an authentic Caesar but an adaptation. A real winner which I stole from the version served at Arizona 206 in New York, when Brendan Walsh was at the stove.

For the dressing
1/4 tsp salt
1/4 tsp coarse-ground black pepper
2 tbl white wine vinegar
2 tbl fresh lemon juice
1 clove garlic, peeled and crushed
1/2 tsp Dijon mustard
1 tsp Worcestershire sauce
2 anchovies, minced
1 egg yolk

1/2 cup (4 fl oz/125 ml) virgin olive oil

1 chipotle en adobe, minced
2 chive stalks, snipped
1 head cos/romaine lettuce, leaves torn in half only
1/2 cup (2 1/2 oz/60 g) crispy fried bacon, diced
1/2 cup (2 1/2 oz/60 g) fresh Parmesan cheese, grated
1 cup (5 oz/125 g) croutons – cut crusty bread into 1/4-inch cubes and marinate in garlic-oil for 30 minutes; then saute over regular heat until crisp and brown

Mix the dressing ingredients together in a large bowl until it becomes frothy. You may use a Robo-Cop or food processor, but don't expect me to love you. Drizzle in the oil and keep blending. Add the chipotle and chives, keep blending for 3 minutes.

Add the lettuce and toss, coat thoroughly then add the bacon, cheese and croutons. Mix thoroughly and serve immediately.

Cobb Salad

This is the messiest, most worthless dish going. And I love it. It was invented by Robert Cobb, the owner of Hollywood's Brown Derby. In usual restaurateur fashion he tried to use up extra or maybe unwanted products. The key is to make sure no ingredient is recognizable.

¹/₂ head iceberg
¹/₂ head romaine lettuce
2 cups (10 oz/250 g) watercress
¹/₂ cup (4 fl oz/125 ml) Kenny's Ranch Dressing (see p.38)

For the dressing
2 ribs celery, finely diced
1 tbl cilantro leaves, chopped

1 red jalapeño, de-seeded, de-veined and finely diced
1 avocado, mashed
1 beefsteak tomato, chopped
1 chicken breast, cooked and diced
2 hard-boiled eggs, grated
¹/₂ cup (2 ¹/₂ oz/60 g) smoked ham,
¹/₃ cup (2 oz/45 g) blue cheese, crumbled

Tear all the leaves until they are tiny. Mix well and refrigerate. Mix all the dressing ingredients and keep at room temperature. Take ¹/₂ cup (4 fl oz/125 ml) Kenny's Ranch Dressing and mix in the lettuce – mix well. Add the dressing and stir into the lettuce mixture. Serve in a bowl or bowls, and I suggest garnishing with snipped chives and crumbled crisp bacon.

The Chef Salad

This is a tossed salad common to many restaurants from Alaska to Florida. It is a protein-rich meal and, as its name suggests, can be made with anything. The common conception is the need for ham, turkey, cheese and boiled eggs. But hey, I'm a chef and I hate turkey and hard-boiled eggs. Executed properly, as used to be the case at the Bar Room in the Four Seasons Hotel, New York, it can be a perfect warm-weather meal. They served the salad with a tuna-flavored dressing, which I've copied here for you. Just embrace your Chef Salad with gusto. Experiment, touch and savour, is what I say.

3 heads of different lettuces, washed and torn into bite-size pieces
2 cups (10 oz/250 g) stemmed watercress
2 scallion stalks, chopped, including whites
1/2 cup (2 1/2 oz/60 g) smoked chicken, chopped
1/2 cup (2 1/2 oz/60 g) smoked ham
5 slices salami
1 cup (5 oz/125 g) smoked cheese, grated

1 tbl Parmesan cheese, grated
1 cup (8 fl oz/250 ml) Salsa Fresca (see p. 15)
1 tbl snipped chives
1/2 cup (2 1/2 oz/125 g) zucchini, finely diced
1/4 cup (1 1/4 oz/30 g) roast corn kernels
8 black olives, pitted and sliced
1 red jalapeño, de-seeded, de-veined and finely diced

Toss the lettuce and watercress in the tuna dressing (see below). Mix the scallions, chicken, ham, salami and cheese, then toss with the lettuce mix. Portion on plates and keep the lettuces high.

Mix the remaining ingredients together. Top each plated salad with the mix and serve – the mix will fall off – but this is cool.

Tuna Dressing

4 egg yolks

1 tsp Dijon mustard

1 tsp red wine vinegar

1/2 tsp kosher salt

1/2 tsp coarse-ground black pepper

1 tbl olive oil

1 6oz/150 g tin of tuna, with oil

1 tbl sour cream

juice of 1 lemon

Whisk all ingredients together and keep at room temperature.

Crab Louis

Where Crab Louis comes from is anyone's guess. San Francisco probably, although Portland and Oregon have both made claims. But who cares? It makes for a cool salad dressing, which works for lobster and shrimp, as it obviously does for crab. The important aspects are a decent salad and top-grade crabmeat. Dungeness Crabs are the most popular western US crabs. They are caught from Alaska to the Baja peninsula in Mexico. They are a typical large rock crab. To make this salad properly, you need Dungeness crabs or brown crabs.

My Louis Dressing

1/4 cup (2 1/2 fl oz/60 ml) double cream

1 cup (8 fl oz/250 ml) mayonnaise (see below)

1/4 cup (2 1/2 fl oz/60 ml) sweet chile dipping sauce

1 tbl lemon juice

1/2 tsp celery salt

1/2 tsp cayenne pepper

1 small green bell pepper, cored and finely diced

6 green olives, pitted and diced

3 heads mixed lettuces, washed and torn apart

3 oz/75 g crabmeat per portion

3 plum tomatoes, cored and diced

3 scallion stalks, chopped

Mix all together and portion. A coddled quail's egg placed on top of each salad and gently sliced, allowing the egg yolk to run out, is cool.

Mayonnaise

In 1912 Richard Hellmann bottled mayonnaise sauce in his New York deli. You probably recognize the name. The American FDA requires that mayonnaise must contain no less than 65 per cent vegetable oil — one reason why you have to make it at home.

1 tsp vinegar
pinch of salt
pinch of ground white pepper
1 egg yolk
1 tbl Dijon mustard
1 ½ cups (12 fl oz/375 ml) olive oil

1 tbl boiling water
1 tbl snipped chives
1 large shallot, diced – squeeze out all the juice
lemon juice

Mix the vinegar, salt, pepper, egg yolk and mustard in small bowl with a whisk. Slowly add the oil. When ³/₄ of the oil has been added, pour in 1 tbl of cold court-bouillon. Continue to drizzle in the oil until it's finished. Add the boiling water and mix…add more cold court-bouillon, if needed, to ensure your have a silky sauce. Refrigerate for 1 hour. Mix in the chives and shallots, then flavor with lemon juice. Taste for seasoning, then chill.

Fiesta Salad

This is my version of a rather ubiquitous Tex-Mex dish often called a taco salad. I like the idea of meats and lettuces served in a deep-fried flour tortilla, but I hate the taco salads we now see nearly everywhere. As a result, I've updated the dish and renamed it. This is served with the fast chili and guacamole recipes below and a little Jalapeño Oil (see p. 34). Make the dressing first or yesterday. It needs time to infuse.

For the salad

3 plum tomatoes, quartered

1 avocado, peeled and carefully diced

1 red bell pepper, roasted, peeled, cored and diced

1 yellow bell pepper, roasted, peeled, cored and diced

1 red jalapeño, de-seeded, de-veined and finely diced

1 radicchio, torn into tiny pieces

1 oak leaf, torn in half

1 endive, leaves left as whole as possible

1 batavia, leaves torn into small pieces

For the dressing

1 small red onion, finely diced

1 tbl cilantro leaves, coarsely chopped

1 clove garlic, finely diced

1 tbl chives, snipped

1 tsp mustard seeds

1 tsp dry mustard, mixed into a paste with a little oil

1 cup (8 fl oz/250 ml) olive oil

1 tbl white wine vinegar

6 12-inch Flour Tortillas (see p. 85)

peanut oil for deep-frying

a few cilantro leaves for garnish

Mix all the dressing ingredients well and keep in a dark cupboard for ate least 12 hours. Combine the salad ingredients, apart from the lettuce leaves, and set to one side. Individually dccp-fry the tortillas, with a heavy weight, like a ladle, held down in the centre of the tortilla. (You want to create a vase-like shape.) Fry four of the tortillas this way for about 1 minute or until crispy. Take the two remaining tortillas, slice them into strips and then broil or fry until brown. Reserve for decoration.

Drizzle jalapeño oil around your plate. Centre a small mound of Fast Guacamole (see below) and place a tortilla on top. Along with ensuring your shell doesn't shoot off the plate, when carried to the table, the guacamole also gives an extra little boost of flavor toward the end of the meal.

Mix the lettuces together and toss in the dressing. Add the other vegetables and toss again. Share the salad amongst the tortilla bowls. Centre a heaped tablespoon of the Cheap Chili (see below) and top with the tortilla strips. Place a couple of cilantro leaves on the strips and dust with Kenny's French Quarter Seasoning (see p. 22).

Cheap Chili

peanut oil
8 oz/185 g ground beef – not lean
1 cup (8 fl oz/250 ml) chicken stock
1 small white onion
1 garlic clove, minced

2 medium tomatoes, diced
2 green jalapeños, de-seeded, de-veined and finely diced
1 tbl My Chili Seasoning (p. 25)
½ cup (4 fl oz/125 ml) red wine

Over moderate heat warm enough oil to cover the bottom of a 10-inch skillet. Add the ground beef and brown. Keep dropping in little amounts of chicken stock if it begins to stick to your pan. Browning should take 5-10 minutes – depending upon your skillet and what you take for moderate heat.

Add the rest of the ingredients, except the stock and wine, and cook for 15 minutes. I presume you realize the need to keep on stirring. Transfer to a baking tray and add the stock and red wine. Place in a pre-heated 350°F/180°C/gas mark 4 oven. Leave for at least 30 minutes before serving.

Fast Guacamole

2 avocados, peeled, pitted and coarsely mashed
2 tomatoes, coarsely chopped
1 scallion, finely chopped

1 tbl cilantro leaves, coarsely chopped
1 tsp My Chili Seasoning (see p. xx)
pinch of ground cumin

Mix all ingredients with a wooden spoon – a metal one will speed up discoloration – and chill until needed.

Tortilla Salad

This salad can be used as a side order or, as I prefer, a substantial, yet cute, garnish on a chicken dinner. Yellow corn chips are of course the norm but you can buy blue chips made from a blue variety of maize. The way to cheat is to put red and then blue vegetable dye in to your base tortilla mix.

6 blue corn tortillas
6 yellow corn tortillas
6 red corn tortillas
peanut oil
1/2 cup (2 1/2 oz/60 g) black beans, cooked
1/2 cup (2 1/2oz/60 g) red bell pepper, finely diced
1/2 cup (2 1/2 oz/60 g) carrot matchsticks

1/2 cup (2 1/2 oz/60 g) yellow bell pepper, finely diced
1/2 cup (2 1/2 oz/60 g) zucchini sticks
4 tbl corn oil
juice of 1/2 lime
1 tbl cilantro leaves
1 jalapeño, finely diced
sea salt and pepper

Cut the tortillas into thin strips. If you take your time they will dry out. (You can cut them quickly by stacking them on top of each other.) Slowly fry small batches of the strips in peanut oil, at around 325°F/170°C. Cook for a maximum of 30 seconds or until crisp. Remove and drain on a paper towel.

Mix the beans with all the vegetables. Add the corn oil, a few dashes of fresh lime juice, the cilantro leaves and the jalapeño. Toss together, then sprinkle with sea salt and crack over two turns of black pepper.

Place gently on top of the tortilla strips and mix carefully – we don't want any broken tortillas. Ensure all the salad is coated then serve immediately – it won't work otherwise.

Cactus and Pear Salad

A native of the New World tropics, the prickly pear is the fruit of the opuntia cactus. They're the ones with flat spiny joints commonly referred to as bunny ears. It was first mentioned in print as long ago as 1612 and is still used in salads, jams, jellies and pickles. (One year my love of cacti took me to Kingsville, Texas. Between the 4th and 6th of April they hold a Prickly Pear and Cactus Festival – where's my anorak?)

You can serve this salad on the side with grilled chicken.

For the salad
2 cups (10 oz/250 g) stemmed watercress
1 small red bell pepper, roasted, peeled,
cored and diced
1 small yellow bell pepper, sliced into very
thin juliennes
4 large ripe plums, pitted and sliced very
thin
5 prickly pears, peeled, mashed and strained
2 ripe pears, peeled, cored and diced

For the dressing
¼ cup (2 ½ fl oz/60 ml) rice wine vinegar
1 cup (8 fl oz 250 ml) olive oil
3 tbl soy sauce
½ tbl sesame oil
3 tbl fresh lime juice
1 red onion, finely chopped
1 clove garlic, minced
1 small red chile
1 tsp fresh mint, chopped
pinch of onion salt
pinch of coarse-ground black pepper

Gently toss all the salad ingredients in a large bowl. Combine all the dressing ingredients and keep at room temperature for 1 hour. Pour the dressing on to the salad ingredients and gently toss. Remove from the bowl and strain for 2 minutes. Ensure the pears and plums are on top when you serve.

The Tohono O'odham ('desert people') Indians, from the Sonora desert, revere the fruit of the 40-foot saguaro cactus — the largest cactus in the US. Why? Because they drink fermented saguaro syrup as 'the earth drinks rain'.

Fried Chicken Salad

Warm salads are a relatively new trend. The most enjoyable one I have recently eaten was at Jan Birnbaum's Catahoula Restaurant & Saloon, California. A charismatic chef, he serves southern-inspired food, with recipes such as skirt steak salad with mushroom and chipotle aioli. He marinates the steak in beer for 8 hours and serves assorted wild mushrooms in the salad — producing a fresh version of the traditional beef dinner. Read this whole recipe thoroughly before starting. The recipe for the fried chicken follows below.

2 cups sliced fried chicken breasts (see recipe below)
snipped chives for garnish
Kenny's French Quarter Seasoning (see p. 22)

For the salad
1/2 carrot, peeled and cut into fine juliennes
1/2 small zucchini, topped and tailed and julienned
1 small red bell pepper seeded, de-veined and julienned
1 small yellow bell pepper seeded, de-veined and julienned
1 small green bell pepper seeded, de-veined and julienned

1 cup (5 oz/125 g) cooked black beans
1 head of endive, leaves torn in half
For the dressing
2 cups (16 fl oz/500 ml) chicken stock
4 ancho chiles, re-hydrated, de-seeded and diced
1 small red onion, diced
2 cloves garlic, minced
1/4 cup (1 1/4 oz/30 g) cilantro leaves, chopped
1/3 cup (3 fl oz/75 ml) honey
1/4 cup (2 1/2 fl oz/60 ml) cider vinegar
1/2 cup (4 fl oz/125 ml) olive oil
1 tbl fresh lime juice
1/2 tsp celery salt
1/2 tsp coarse-ground black pepper

Gently toss all the salad ingredients in a large bowl and then refrigerate.

Bring the chicken stock to boil and add the anchos, onion, garlic and cilantro. Cook for 10 minutes. Pour into a blender and puree for 3 minutes. Add the honey and vinegar and blend for a further 2 minutes, then slowly drizzle in the oil until it is well incorporated. Turn the blender off and mix in the lime juice and seasoning. Keep at room temperature.

Immediately remove the vegetables from the fridge and toss with the warm fried chicken and the ancho dressing. Centre the salad on the plates, ensuring the chicken is visible and that it is shared equally. Sprinkle snipped chives around the plate and dust with Kenny's French Quarter Seasoning. Enjoy.

Fried Chicken for a salad

For the batter
1 ¹/₂ cups (7 ¹/₂ oz/185 g) all-purpose flour
¹/₂ cup (4 fl oz/125 ml) buttermilk
2 eggs, beaten
1 tbl Louisiana Hot Sauce
¹/₂ tbl oregano
1 tbl snipped chives
1 tbl olive oil

For the cornmeal dip
pinch of baking powder
1 cup (5 oz/125 g) cornmeal
1 tsp paprika
¹/₂ tsp garlic salt
¹/₂ tsp ground white pepper

5 chicken supremes, sliced into thin strips and dusted with Kenny's French Quarter Seasoning (see p. 22)
peanut oil for frying

Combine all ingredients for the batter and whisk well. Mix together all the ingredients for the cornmeal dip. With one hand dip the chicken in the batter. With the same hand remove and drop in cornmeal mix. Still with the same hand make sure the chicken is coated. Repeat with each piece and chill for 10 minutes – this helps the coating stay on. Then shallow fry for 2–3 minutes in oil heated to 375°F/190°C.

SANDWICHES AND THEIR FRIENDS

SANDWICHES and THEIR FRIENDS

Breads

Increasingly, folk are coming round to the notion that it is the bread that maketh the sandwich. Hallelujah! Consequently the bread business is now big business. Noel Comess of the Tom Cat Bakery and Eli Zabar of Eli's Bread in New York have developed multi-million dollar businesses in serving the leisure industry and many restaurants now attach a bakery and deli to their premises to make the most of their freshly baked produce.

Nancy Silverton has also made a fortune out of writing about and cooking wonderfully flavored breads with such recipes as seeded sourdough, rustic olive herb, chocolate sour cherry and fig anise breads.

Making bread, for me, is a divine sensory experience that reinforces the kitchen as the heart and soul of the home. The yeast and baking smells alone make these recipes worth pursuing. To bake your own bread you must follow some basic rules, but after that the world is your loaf.

What follows are some of my own inventions for sandwich bread. All the recipes follow the basic principles of My Own White Loaf on p. 55, with just a few nuances.

Sally Lunn

Sally Lunn is a bread made with lemon juice and honey. It's finished with a sugar glaze. Despite being of English origin, recipes for Sally Lunn are found throughout 19th-century American cookbooks.

Walnut Breakfast Bread

This is great for eating with ham and eggs. Incorporate walnut oil, chopped walnuts and sour cream into your basic bread.

Zucchini Bread

This is my favorite enriched bread – soft brown sugar, chopped walnuts, grated zucchini and orange zest are the main players.

Anadama Bread

This is made from cornmeal and molasses. It is one of the earliest American breads.

Parker House Rolls

This is a puffy yeast roll created at the Parker House Hotel in Boston, soon after its opening in 1855. It is famous for its unique folds (a creased center like a purse) and delicate flavor. The key ingredients are honey and butter.

But in the end who needs a recipe? A willingness to experiment is the real key. That's it for bread. Have fun.

Dining Out Stateside

The Americans, if not inventors of fast food and the democratic meal, certainly made it their own and sold it back to the world. Yet McDonald's and Kentucky Fried Chicken are a pale imitation of the great family-run blue-collar eateries that gave birth to them: the delis of the Jewish ghettos and the diners and lunch counters which fed the cities that never sleep. They were the antithesis of fast food today, providing hearty and lovingly prepared home-cooked food in unpretentious surroundings. Many of the diners and delis sprung out of the needs of a particular immigrant community, whether it be kosher food for the Middle-European Jews or soulfood for black migrants from the South.

The Second Avenue Deli in Manhattan is supposed to be *the* deli, with it's chopped liver, matzo ball soup and corned beef – all kosher. My personal favorite is Rein's Deli up in Vernon, Connecticut. It's at exit 65-66 off I-84 just north of Hartford, where they have a friendly immigration centre. After gorging yourself on boiled brisket, take home some frozen home-made soup and some bialys – baked rolls sprinkled with onion flakes.

Deli owners know how to get your juices flowing. Not only through their tempting displays of food but also with their great names for everything. At the Carnegie Deli in Manhattan 'whiskey down' means toasted rye bread, 'nervous pudding' is jello, 'first lady' is spareribs.

At the lunch counter (as the name suggests this is a laid-back blue-collar diner serving unpretentious food at a counter), they too know the art of selling a meal – 'Adam and Eve on a raft' is two poached eggs on toast, 'city juice' is water, 'hold the nail' means no ice, and 'zeppelins in a fog' is what you call sausages in mashed potatoes.

Another of the great fast food pioneers was the classic American diner. Whether the on-the-block lunch-counter type made famous by Edward Hopper or those mobile silver streamlined trailers that parked in lots from Arizona to New Jersey, they had a common purpose. Diners were the original venue for 24-hour fast, filling meals. Their main clientele was often the nightshift. The first was set up by Walter Scott in 1872 in Providence, Rhode Island. There are still an estimated 2,500 old-style diners in operation around the world. Most no longer serve their original community and have been corralled for their retro-novelty value yet the food remains the same.

Whilst on the subject of low-key service establishments that originated in the States, it is important to mention the soda fountain. Carbonated water, often flavored and colored, was sold from the late 1700s, and soon after specially made parlours called soda fountains were set up for this sole purpose. Soon sweeteners and flavors like ginger beer were being added to the sodas and the term 'pop' was coined for the drink, the sound the soda bottle made when opening. I guess you know where all this ended up?

In 1886 Dr John Smyth Pemberton, a pharmacist in Atlanta, Georgia, produced a soda drink flavoured with extracts of kola nut and the leaf of the cocoa plant. This drink was trademarked in 1893 as Coca-Cola. In 1898 a similar product was produced in New Bern, North Carolina by another pharmacist Caleb Bradham. His drink became known in 1903 as Pepsi-Cola. And I guess the rest is history. I would like to guess how many zillions of gallons of these products have been dispensed by fast-food joints, ball parks and restaurants since.

The soda fountain has secured mythical status in American culture – from the paintings of Norman Rockwell to the jukebox generation – as the place where clean-cut, cooing teenagers would meet up to stare longingly at each other over a soda. Elliston Place Soda Shop close to the Vanderbilt Univerity in Nashville, Tennessee is a perfectly preserved 1950s style soda shop – and well worth a visit. Make sure you save room for their banana split.

In my experience it is not only kids who enjoy a banana sandwich filled with three ice creams, three sauces, whipped cream and a sickly garnish, but, if I was to eat this type of dessert I would defintely go for the more traditional Banana Cream Pie.

Banana Cream Pie

For the chocolate cookie crust
1 1/4 cups (6 1/4 oz/155 g) crushed chocolate digestive cookies
1/4 cup (1 1/4 oz/30 g) unsalted butter, melted

For the filling
3 egg yolks
3/4 cup (3 3/4 oz/90 g) sugar
3 tbl cornstarch

1/4 tsp salt
1 1/2 cups (12 fl oz/125 ml) milk
1 tbl unsalted butter
1 tsp vanilla extract – I'll let you work out why vanilla extract is in so many dessert recipes
1/2 cup (4 fl oz/125 ml) double cream
3 ripe bananas, peeled and thinly sliced

To make the crust, pre-heat the oven to 375°F/190°C/gas mark 5. Mix the cookies with the butter. Press the mix over the base of a 9-inch pie tin. Bake the crust for 5 minutes and allow to completely cool.

Beat the egg yolks, add the sugar, cornstarch and salt – mix. Stir in the milk. Add the butter and transfer to a saucepan. (Use a rubber spatula to ensure your mixing bowl doesn't keep some of the mix for itself.) Cook over a medium heat for 5 minutes or until the mix begins to bubble. Make sure the butter is melted.

Remove the pan from the heat and mix in the vanilla. Transfer what is now a custard to a glass bowl, tightly cover, pressing the cling film on to the custard – this stops a skin forming. Refrigerate for a couple of hours. Or until it stops wobbling.

Whip the cream until peaks form. Fold the cream into the custard, take it easy but ensure it is thoroughly mixed. Layer half the bananas over the top of the crust. Mix the remaining bananas into the top of the custard. Spoon the custard over the crust, seal with cling film and refrigerate overnight.

To garnish use one or more of the following: more cream, caramelized bananas, pecans, chocolate flakes. Serve with a smile

Soda fountain beverages – be they ice cream floats, flips, malts, milkshakes or Coca-Cola – are the traditional drink to be served with that other great American invention – the burger ...

The Burger

The question of the humble burger's origins is highly contentious and shrouded in mystery by claims and counter-claims. Suffice it to say this quintessential proletarian sandwich really began its journey to stardom when McDonald's opened in Des Plaines, Illinois in 1955. The original ideal, however, has very little in common with the omnipresent version we see in our high streets. (Don't you hate all those discarded wrappers?)

John Mariani puts it plain and simply in his glorious *Dictionary of American Food and Drink*: 'The burger is a grilled, fried or broiled patty of ground beef...' Yet within this prosaic definition lie a thousand arguments about just what makes the perfect patty. In my book the burger should not be restricted to just ground beef. Lamb, chicken, fish, venison and even pulses can be formed into a 'burger' and I welcome them, one and all. Here are my favorites.

The condiments are just a guide, but I seriously suggest making your own burger buns – your guests will be mighty impressed. Nothing is worse than having a lovingly produced patty ruined by a lousy piece of bread.

My Home Burger

For the patties (enough for 4)
4 cups (1 1/2 lb/600 g) minced sirloin
1 tbl olive oil
1 cup (5 oz/125 g) red onion, grated
1 egg, beaten
1 tbl dry mustard
2 tsp Worcestershire sauce

1 tsp creamed horseradish
1 tsp Louisiana Hot Sauce
1 tsp coarse-ground black pepper
1/2 tsp garlic salt
1/2 cup (2 1/2 oz/60 g) fresh cilantro leaves,
chopped

Mix all the ingredients together with your hands. Get messy. Form into 8oz/185 g patties. Wash your hands. Broil or barbecue to your liking.

   I like to serve my burgers with batavia lettuce and mayonnaise on one side of the toasted bun and ketchup on the other. But it is really up to you, I guess. French fries have to go with a burger and that's about all, except for ice cold beer. Miller Genuine Draft is my preference – it's 'Miller time!'.

French Fries

6 large Maris Piper potaotes
1 1/4 cups (6 oz/150 g) all-purpose flour
peanut oil at 375°F/190°C for deep-frying

2 tbl Kenny's French Quarter Seasoning (see
p. 22)

Cut the potatoes into sixths. Soak in cold water for about 30 minutes. Drain. Dust in flour and fry for 10 minutes. Let the potatoes cool on kitchen roll for a few minutes, then dust and shake with the seasoning.

Smoked Chicken Burger

Mark Erickson, Executive Chef at the Cherokee Town and Country Club in Atlanta, Georgia, inspired this dish with his Southern Fried Chicken Burger. He chooses honey-mustard mayonnaise and toasted peanut and sweet corn salad as his accompaniment. My preferred choice is mushroom ketchup, beer-braised onions or a southwestern green chili sauce. This is enough for 4 patties.

1 ¹/₄ lb/550 g 'pulled' smoked or roast chicken meat – I suggest dark and white meat

1 egg, beaten

3 tbl buttermilk

1 clove garlic, minced

1 tsp sea salt

1 tsp ground white pepper

1 tsp coarse-ground black pepper

1 ¹/₄ cups (6 oz/150 g) breadcrumbs

'Pulled' chicken just means off the bone and finger shredded. Mix all the ingredients by hand, and add the chicken meat.

The Definitive Burger Bun

Beware – this is not a short recipe, but is definitely one worth attempting. A sourdough bun may sound odd but it makes a worthy partner for a great burger. Sourdough is one of the oldest forms of bread. This recipe, ideally, will make 12 burger buns.

For the yeast mix

2 packs dried yeast

2 cups (16 fl oz/500 ml) warm water

1 tsp sugar

2 cups (10 oz/250 g) wholewheat flour

For the dough

3 ¹/₂ cups (1 lb 2 ¹/₂ oz/510 g) wholewheat

flour

3 cups (1 lb/450 g) all-purpose flour

1 tbl salt

1 tbl brown sugar

¹/₂ tsp baking powder

¹/₂ tsp bicarbonadate of soda

¹/₂ tsp sugar

To make the yeast mix: mix the yeast into the water. Sprinkle in the sugar and leave until frothy. Whisk in the flour. Leave at room temperature for 24 hours or more. We want the batter to ferment and then die down.

To make the dough: mix the two flours together. Sift 3 cups (1 lb/450 g) of the flours with the other ingredients. Add 1 cup (8 fl oz/250 ml) of the yeast mix. Mix well, cover and leave at room temperature for 24 hours. You can keep the yeast mix alive by adding flour and water. This way it will last for ages. Or you can just discard it.

Next day, add the remaining flour to the dough and pour in $^{3}/_{4}$ cup (6 fl oz/175 ml) water. Knead well, until you have a soft dough. Roll the dough into 3-inch balls, place on a greased baking tray, cover with a damp cloth and leave to rise for 2–4 hours.

Pre-heat the oven to 425°F/220°C/gas mark 7. Brush the tops of the buns with salted water. With a razor cut slashes across the top. Dust with flour. Bake for 8 minutes, then turn the temperature down to 400°F/200°C/gas mark 6 and bake for 25 minutes.

Mushroom Ketchup

My favorite burger condiment. This is a steal from Carlyn Berghoff Catering in Chicago, although I omitted the hot beer that they like to use. I like to keep mine cool.

1 red onion, finely diced
2 tbl unsalted butter
1 1/2 cups (7 1/2 oz/185 g) strong-flavored
mushrooms, sliced
1 tbl cider vinegar

1/2 cup (4 fl oz/125 ml) tomato ketchup,
preferably home-made
1 tbl brown sugar
1/2 tsp salt

Saute the onion in the butter until soft. Add the mushrooms and vinegar. Cook until the vinegar has disappeared and take off the heat. Add the remaining ingredients and mix well. Allow to cool then transfer to a Mason jar or similar container. Seal and keep in a dark cupboard for at least 24 hours before use.

Beer-braised Onions

Beer and onions is a classic American combination. I use dark beer like Guinness or San Francisco's wonderful Anchor Steam.

3 white onions, sliced
2 tbl unsalted butter
1 15 fl oz/440ml can of dark beer
2 scallions, diced

1 clove garlic, finely diced
1 tsp sugar
1 tsp Pepper Seasoning (see p. 24)

Over a moderate heat saute the onions in the butter for 5 minutes. You will need to keep stirring. Add the rest of the ingredients and cook over a low heat for 20 minutes or until most of the beer has evaporated. Keep warm.

Green Chile Burger Sauce

This sauce is delicate and fresh-flavored – perfect for those warm summer days. Do not add tomatoes, leave that to the Texans. In the south-west we use tomatillos. This is a recipe similar to the green chile sauce you'll find at El Cholo in Los Angeles.

8 green jalapeños, roasted, peeled, de-seeded
1 tsp oregano
2 cloves garlic, finely diced
1 1/2 cups (12 fl oz/375 ml) chicken stock

1 cup (5 oz/125 g) tomatillo meat
1/2 cup (4 fl oz/125 ml) sour cream –
more if you want to dilute the spiciness

Simmer the jalapeños, oregano and garlic in the stock for 20 minutes. Let cool then pour into a blender. Add the tomatillos and puree for 2 minutes. Return to your pot and bring to a simmer. Keep warm. Just before serving add the sour cream. Let your guests pour the sauce over their burgers themselves.

White Chili Smothering Sauce

Chili burgers are increasingly popular and this is my favorite smothering sauce. I tend to eat this just as often without the burger. Chili burgers are a favorite in Minneapolis which due, I guess, to its seriously low winter temperatures, has developed something of a hot food culture. Its Loon Cafe produces a Pecos River Red XX chili which will blow off your cowboy boots long before you make it to your burger. This recipe is slightly tamer.

1 large onion, coarsely chopped

2 tbl peanut oil

6 cups (2 lb/900 g) pulled chicken meat

1/2 cup (2 1/2 oz/60 g) diced red jalapeños, seeds included

1 tsp cayenne pepper

1 tsp paprika

1 tbl crushed red peppers

1 tsp ground cumin

1 tsp oregano

2 cups (10 oz/250 g) tinned tomatoes, crushed

2 cups (16 fl oz/500 ml) chicken stock

1 tbl cornflour, mixed with 1 tbl of water

Saute the onion in the oil until soft. Add the rest of the ingredients, except the flour paste, and bring to a simmer. Add the paste and mix in well. Cook for 20 minutes, then keep warm before serving. Smother your burger with the chili and chow down.

Here's some more useful burger terminology: you may hear your guests asking for 'the works', this means they want it all – ketchup, pickles, relishes, sauerkraut etc. – American folk love excess. If they want you to 'drag it through the garden', this means plenty of lettuce and salad.

Santa Fe Grilled Cheese Sandwich

The greatest American sandwich is supposed to be a 4-inch high BLT. I disagree. Nothing really beats a grilled cheese sandwich, especially one with some added south-western passion.

2 tbl unsalted butter
4 slices of your favorite bread
²/₃ cup (4 oz/100 g) sharp Cheddar cheese, grated
2 tbl sour cream
1 avocado, sliced

2 tsp chipotle puree (puree an 8 oz /185 g can of chipotle en adobe with lime juice and a little oil)
½ red onion, sliced
2 tbl cilantro leaves

I guess you can work out how to make the sandwich. The only tricks are to butter both sides of the bread and to broil both sides – a flat top works best for this. I like to bring the sandwich to the table open faced. This way I can serve them straight from under the broiler, with the cheese molten hot and the other ingredients, hiding underneath, just slightly warm.

Cuban Cheese Sandwich

This Hispanic sandwich is a religion. It is made with Cuban bread which is made with olive oil, yeast and less flour than the average loaf. It is a little like French bread but lighter and flatter. It should be 5–8 inches long. The bread is cut diagonally, spread with yellow mustard and layered with thin slices of roast pork, ham, Genoa salami, Swiss cheese and sliced dill pickle. If you ever come across it, say at the Valencia Garden Restaurant in Tampa, Florida, ask for it 'pressed'. This is when the sandwich is brushed with pork drippings and heated in a fold-down press.

Debris Po'boy

The po'boy is a southern incarnation of the classic American sandwich, a near relative of the hoagy or the hero. It is traditionally made with leftovers, hence the name (poor boy). A debris po'boy is simply a large baguette smothered with all the drippings and loose meats from your Sunday roast – beef, pork or lamb. I cheat a little and include all the end pieces of the roast, which always appear to mysteriously fall off during carving. It is a wonderfully messy sandwich. I defy you to eat it without having rivers of juice working their way down your chin and on to your favorite Ralph Lauren shirt. If you're ever in town, the finest debris po'boys are to be found at Mother's in New Orleans.

Rueben Sandwich

This famous sandwich supposedly originated at the late Rueben's Deli on 58th Street in Manhattan. Or it may have been created by Rueben Kulakovsky at the Blackstone Hotel in Omaha, Nebraska. I don't really care which is true. Either way it has become a major player in the American sandwich psyche. It has to be made with real corned beef, Swiss cheese, rye bread, sauerkraut and Russian dressing. It needs to be broiled.

For your Rueben, you need to smother seeded rye bread with Russian dressing. Layer pastrami, sauerkraut and Gruyere cheese and then top with another slice of bread.

Heat some unsalted butter in a skillet. Brown each side of the sandwich. Cut in half and serve.

Pastrami, by the way, is corned beef which has been dried, rubbed with coarse pepper and spices, smoked over hardwood sawdust and then steamed. The name comes from the Romanian word for 'preserve'. Langers on St Alvarado St in Downtown LA offers copious deli classics such as chopped liver, gefilte fish, blintzes and lox. It's in a bad neighborhood, and has a lousy atmosphere, but the food's great. How many joints can boast 27 different pastrami dishes?

Coney Island Red Hots

Coney Island in Brooklyn, along with being home to a great amusement park and the best pizza pie (at Totonno Pizzeria Napoletano on Neptune Avenue), is also responsible for one of America's most famous sandwiches. It is an original hot dog (a white frankfurter) with all the trappings and topped with chili. A true ball park special.

2 onions, finely chopped
2 tbl peanut oil
6 hot dog buns
unsalted butter

French mustard
6 frankfurters
3 cups (1 lb/450 g) chili

Saute the onions in the oil until they are soft. Keep warm. Split the buns, but not all the way through. Lightly toast them. Butter the insides and then spread a little mustard over the butter. Add the frankfurter and top with chili. Smother with onions and serve immediately. You now need a cold beer.

Sloppy Joe

This is a dish of ground beef — chili style, with ketchup in the mix — served over a hamburger roll or just plain. It is sloppy to eat and a genuine article. If the sandwich doesn't drip, it's not authentic. For their Sloppy Joe, Ed Debevic's in Beverly Hills only uses medium-ground prime beef and it tastes great despite the side order of molded gelatin salad! Ed Debevic's house speciality is listed as 'fine service'.

Simply saute onions and green bell peppers together until the onion is soft. Add some diced jalapeños and garlic and cook for a little longer. In the mix brown your ground beef. Once browned add My Chili Seasoning (see p. 25), ketchup and crushed tomatoes. Cook until you have a thick sauce. Serve over toasted buns.

Potato Salad

Tribeca, Manhattan's triangle below Canal Street, once the site of America's largest commercial food market, is now the home to some of the country's finest restaurants. Nosmo King, the Odeon, Duane Park Cafe and the famous Tribeca Grill.

The following recipe is inspired by chef Seiji Maeda of the Duane Park Cafe. Serve on the side of all your favorite sandwiches.

1 cup (8 fl oz/250 ml) virgin olive oil
¼ cup (2 fl oz/60 ml) balsamic vinegar
1 tsp salt
½ tsp coarse-ground black pepper
12 button mushrooms, sliced
2 tbl olive oil
12 sun-dried tomatoes, dropped in boiling

water for 3 minutes, drained and finely chopped
1 tbl fresh sage, finely chopped
1 clove garlic, minced
¾ cup (3 ¾ oz/90 g) parsley, finely chopped
9 cups (3 lb/1.3 kg) Maris Piper potatoes

Combine the virgin oil, vinegar, salt and pepper and whisk together. Set aside for 2 hours. Over a moderate heat saute the mushrooms in the olive oil for 3 minutes. Add the tomatoes, sage, garlic and parsley. Stir well and cook for a further 5 minutes. Keep at room temperature.

Take your potatoes, cut into 2-inch cubes and boil in salted water until tender.

Drain the potatoes and whilst still warm toss in the dressing and tomato mix.

Tuna Melt

Canned tuna comes in for a lot of grief but I stand by it. Buttering on the outside and grilling turns this into the finest of meals. You can use fresh tuna if you want, but it is not really necessary.

1 7 oz/180 g can tuna, drained
1/3 cup (2 oz/45 g) celery, finely chopped
1/4 cup (1 1/4 oz/30 g) onion, finely chopped

3 tbl pimento-stuffed olives, chopped
1/3 cup (3 fl oz/75 ml) mayonnaise
plenty of cheddar cheese

Mix all the ingredients together except the cheese. Pre-heat the oven to 425°F/220°C/gas mark 7. Then take 8 slices of bread, buttered on both sides. Grill both sides until brown. Place the bread on a baking tray. Spread the tuna mix over each piece, then smother in grated Cheddar cheese. Place the tray in the oven and cook until the cheese has melted – about 10 minutes. You can work out how to make 4 sandwiches.

Heroes, Subs and Grinders

Heroes, Submarines, Grinders, Wedges, Hoagies, Zeppelins and Torpedoes. American sandwiches have a whole lot in common with each other and usually involve cold cuts and cheeses, piled on to long bread loaves.

My Meatball 'Hero Boy'

Ideally you should use Italian bread for a Hero. But you can substitute French. The breadneeds to be about 5 inches long by 3 inches wide. I've used beef but any type of meat can be used in this recipe.

1 bread loaf
4 cups (1 ½ lb/600 g) ground beef
1 onion, grated
1 clove garlic, finely diced
1 tsp oregano
1 tsp dry mustard
1 tsp Pepper Seasoning (see p. 24)

1 tbl cilantro leaves, chopped
1 egg, beaten
½ cup (2 ½ oz/60 g) all-purpose flour
2 tbl olive oil
2 cups (16 fl oz/500 ml) My Old-fashioned Tomato Sauce (see p. 117)

Mix all ingredients, except the oil and tomato sauce. Form into smallish balls. Heat the oil and cook the meatballs in batches. Do not allow them to stick. Transfer the meatballs to paper towels and allow to drain. Keep warm.

Heat the tomato sauce. Whilst this is cooking add the meatballs. Cook over a moderate heat for about 15 minutes or until the sauce is thick.

Cut your bread in half and remove some of the centre, otherwise your balls may fall off.

Place 3 meatballs on each bottom and smother with sauce, top with the other half of bread and eat.

The Hoagie is apparently Philadelphia's official sandwich. Lee's Hoagie House, founded in 1953 in the West Oak Lane section of the city, offers a dozen different varieties, the classic being the Italian – pepper ham, genoa salami, cappicola, provolone, lettuce, tomato, onions, hot peppers, spices and oils. It is awesome. I'll let you figure out how to make one.

Macaroni and Cheese

Is he serious ?' I hear you saying. You better believe it. Every American girl I have ever dated has cooked me this dish. Why? Because this dish is embedded in the American psyche, and this is all down to its number one fan – Thomas Jefferson. Despite being a well-travelled gastronaut and having a penchant for growing everything from seed, Jefferson would often serve good ole down-home macaroni pie at the White House.

1 ½ cups (8 oz/185 g) macaroni
¼ cup (1 ¼ oz/30 g) unsalted butter
⅓ cup (2 oz/45 g) all-purpose flour, sieved
½ tsp celery salt
½ tsp dry mustard

¼ tsp ground white pepper
1 tsp hot sauce
2 ½ cups (1 pint/625 ml) milk
2 ½ cups (12 ½ oz/310 g) Cheddar cheese, grated

Cook the pasta as the package directs. Pre-heat the oven to 350°F/180°C/gas mark 4. Butter your baking dish. In a saucepan melt the butter. Stir in the flour, salt, mustard, pepper and hot sauce, until smooth. Gradually stir in the milk; keep stirring until the sauce begins to bubble. Stir in 2 cups (10 oz/250 g) cheese. Cook until the cheese has melted Pour the sauce over the macaroni. Top with the rest of the cheese and bake for 30 minutes or until hot. Most folk garnish with tomato wedges, I prefer cilantro leaves and Salsa Fresca (see p. 15).

Boston Baked Beans

This is the original baked beans recipe. Forget commercial products, make them yourself using salt pork and molasses. A hearty treat.

3 cups (1 lb/450 g) navy beans, soaked in water overnight, boiled in fresh water for 20 minutes, then drained
1 large onion, coarsely chopped
2/3 cup (4 oz/100 g) salt pork, diced

2 tbl brown sugar
1/4 cup (2 1/2 fl oz/60 ml) molasses
2 tsp dry mustard
1 tsp garlic salt
1 tsp coarse-ground black pepper

Pre-heat the oven to 325°F/170°C/gas mark 3. Combine all the ingredients in a casserole dish. Cover with water and bake for 5 hours or until the beans are tender. You will need to stir occasionally and maybe add a little more water to keep the dish moist.

Philly Cheesesteak

This messy sandwich is a way of life. It's the kind of honest feast that tastes best eaten on the streets. Simply saute up a mess of onions. Slice thinly some skirt, eye-round or ribeye steak, and broil. Add some seasonings, mix with the fried onions and stuff in an 8-inch bread roll. Top with some nasty, cheap melted cheese – Cheese Whiz or Provolone is preferable – and enjoy. It is not particularly healthy eating, but mighty fine.

175

Check it out the next time you are in South Philadelphia at Pat's King of Steak at Ninth and Passyunk. Pat's has been owned by the Olivieri family for 65 years. (Mr Frank Sinatra once frequented the joint; probably why they sell more cheesesteaks than anyone else.) A side order of cheese fries, a fountain-made cherry coke and a Tastykake for dessert will give you the ultimate Philadelphia eating experience.

Muffuletta

This is an Italian-American invention from down in New Orleans. I bet you fail to make it happen. You may succeed if you use quality olives, olive oil, cheese and salami. But is it worth it for a sandwich? You bet it is!

For the salad
1 cup (5 oz/125 g) chopped green olives
1 cup (5 oz/125 g) chopped black olives
1/2 cup (4 fl oz/125 ml) olive oil
1/3 cup (2 oz/45 g) cilantro, chopped
1/2 cup (2 1/2 oz/60 g) red bell peppers, roasted, peeled, de-seeded and sliced
2 anchovy fillets, mashed
1 tsp oregano

1 tsp lemon juice
1 tsp cracked black pepper
1 round loaf, about 8 inches in diameter
2 cups (10 oz/250 g) shredded lettuce –
a bitter lettuce like endive is best
1 1/2 cups (7 1/2 oz/185 g) tomatoes, chopped
4 oz/100 g salami, sliced
4 oz/100 g smoked ham, sliced
4 oz/100 g Provolone cheese, sliced

Combine the salad ingredients and refrigerate overnight. Drain in the morning. Cut the bread in half – sideways. In any order, layer the ingredients on the bottom half. Top with other half of bread. Place a plate on top and weigh it down, with, say a bag of flour. Refrigerate for an hour or so. Cut into quarters and serve with the salad.

Pulled Barbecue Pork Sandwich

Butch McQuire's in Chicago offers the finest pork sandwich to be found anywhere. I first met Butch through the late Bob Payton – the hospitality impresario with the big mouth. Here is my own version of the sandwich, although, when 'pulling', I usually eat too much of the meat to leave enough for a decent sandwich. Serve with a side of Potato Slaw (see below) and Boston Baked Beans (see p. 175).

1 2 ½ lb/1.1 kg smoked ham hock
1 tsp garlic salt
2 tbl Louisiana Hot Sauce
1 cup (8 fl oz/250 ml) Razorback Sopping Sauce (see p. 178)
1 medium onion, sliced

1 rib celery, finely diced
1 clove garlic, minced
1 red jalapeño, de-seeded, de-veined and finely diced
½ tsp celery salt
6 sandwich buns

Heat the oven to 325°F/170°C/gas mark 3. Cover the bottom of a casserole dish with a ½ inch of water. Place the hock in the middle of the dish. Sprinkle with the garlic salt and pour over the hot sauce. Carefully pour a ½ cup (4 fl oz/125 ml) of the sopping sauce over the hock. Surround with the vegetables and cover with foil. Cook for 1 hour then turn. Cook for another hour and remove from the oven. Split the hock to the bone and pour over the vegetables and juices. Return to the oven and cook for another hour. Turn the oven off and leave the hock in there for another hour – don't look at it.

When cool, remove from the dish and separate the fat from the meat – do with the fat as you wish. With the tines of the fork start scraping the meat off the bone. This will not take long.

Add the rest of the Sopping Sauce to the juices in the pan and gently heat. While the sauce is heating, toast the buns. Centre the bottom halves of the buns on plates, pile a quarter of the meat on each bun. Spoon over the sauce and top with the other half of the bun. Place Potato Slaw on one side and Boston Baked Beans on the other.

Your guests may be a little surprised at the size of their lunch. I always try to serve my Pulled Sandwiches with pitchers of San Francisco's Anchor Steam beer.

Potato Slaw

This Tennessee recipe combines the best of coleslaw and potato salad. I love its ability to match the robust flavors of barbecued food.

1/4 cup (2 1/2 fl oz/60 ml) mayonnaise
1 tbl Dijon mustard
2 cups (10 oz/250 g) red cabbage, washed and shredded
1/4 cup (1 1/4 oz/30 g) green bell pepper,

cored, de-veined and diced
1/4 cup (1 1/4 oz) cucumber, finely diced
1 tsp garlic salt
1 cup (5 oz/125 g) new potatoes, boiled and diced

Combine all the ingredients, except the potatoes and mix. Add the potatoes and gently mix. Chill for a minimum of 1 hour.

Razorback Sopping Sauce

A sopping sauce does not allude to a habitual drunkard, but is the name for a basting sauce.

Joyce Rogers of Pa and Ma's Barbecue in Indianapolis says the only time to sop is when the meat begins to swell and open up. This ain't necessarily so.

1 cup (8 fl oz/250 ml) water
1/2 cup (4 fl oz/125 ml) cider vinegar
1/2 cup (2 1/2 oz/60 g) unsalted butter
4 tbl brown sugar
1 tsp cracked black pepper
2 tsp salt

1 tsp cayenne pepper
2 tbl coarse-grain mustard
2 medium onions, sliced
4 tbl Worcestershire sauce
1 tbl soy sauce
1 tbl Louisiana hot sauce

Leaving out the Worcestershire, soy and hot sauces, bring the ingredients to a boil and simmer for 20 minutes. Take off the heat and add the other sauces. You are now ready to sop.

Lobster Club Sandwich

Anne Rosenzweig has been one of the most respected chefs in Manhattan for years. This sandwich is always on her lunch menu at Arcadia on East 62nd Street. It is highly regarded.

I have substituted her lemon mayonnaise with my chipotle version and used smoked ham instead of apple-smoked bacon.

I wrote earlier about not having the space to teach you about making bread; this time it is brioche. But I'm sure you can find a recipe. Michael McCarty, of Michael's Restaurants in Santa Monica and New York produces a fine recipe in his cookbook.

For the chipotle mayonnaise
1 cup (8 fl oz/250 ml) Hellmann's
Mayonnaise
1 tbl chipotle en adobe
1 tsp soy sauce
1 tsp lemon juice
1 tsp olive oil

For the sandwich
1 brioche loaf
2 cups (10 oz/250 g) crisp romaine lettuce,
torn into bite-sized pieces
4 slices smoked ham
2 ripe plum tomatoes, sliced
8 oz/185 g cooked, cold lobster tail – slice on
the 'bias' (as Anne says) to a 1/2-inch thick

Combine the mayonnaise ingredients and keep at room temperature. Slice the brioche to your favorite thickness. Toast lightly. Spread the mayo. on two toasted sides. Layer each one with lettuce, ham, tomatoes and lobster. Top with another piece of un-mayoed brioche. Serve mayo side down.

The Monte Cristo

The Monte Cristo is a crisp and crunchy version of the ubiquitous European 'croque monsieur'. It's a grilled cheese sandwich which the Spanish call *emparedados de jamon y queso* and the Italians call *mozzarella en carozza*.

2 tbl coarse-grain mustard	*1 tbl red jalapeños, de-seeded, de-veined*
4 tbl double cream	*and finely diced*
10 slices good thick white bread	*1 tbl snipped chives*
8 oz/185 g Gruyere cheese, thinly sliced	*1/2 cup (2 1/2 oz/60 g) clarified butter*
4 oz/100 g your favorite ham	*3 large eggs, beaten with 1 tsp soy sauce*

Mix the mustard and cream. Lay five slices of bread down and spread the mix on top. Lay the cheese, ham, jalapeños and chives on top. Cover with the other slices. Heat the butter.

Coat the sandwiches in the egg mix (this must be a gentle operation). Place the sandwiches, one at a time, in the butter and fry until golden, turning once. Cut the sandwiches in half and serve with potato chips.

Potato Chips

It is said potato chips originated at Moon's Lake House in Saratoga Springs, Upstate New York. We'll never know, but they are now obviously an enormous part of our fast food culture. I prefer sweet potato chips to the regular baking potato chips.

Peel four small sweet potatoes. Cut into very thin slices. Rinse well in cold water, dry on kitchen paper. Heat your oil to 375°F/190°C and fry the potatoes, without crowding, until crispy. Drain and season.

Hot Browns

This is a sandwich created at Louisville's Brown Hotel. It's funny how simple things become icons. All you need is diced chicken or turkey, broiled bacon, grated fresh Parmesan cheese and a good mornay sauce. Obviously good toasted bread is also needed.

Mix the sauce with the diced meat, spread on bread, sprinkle with Parmesan and garnish with the bacon. Keep the sandwich open-faced and pop under the broiler for 3–4 minutes. You'll need the heat high. Put the bread together and eat before the 'squeeze' comes through.

Mornay Sauce

This sauce is extremely popular. My recipe is based on James Beard's mornay sauce. His books are a must for every avid cook. And as James himself says, 'I urge you to be adventurous'.

1 1/2 cups (12 fl oz/375 ml) Sauce Veloute (see below)
1/2 cup (2 1/2 oz/60 g)Parmesan cheese, grated

1/2 cup (4 fl oz/125 ml) single cream
3 twists of a black pepper mill
3 twists of a koshering or rock salt mill
3 dashes of jalapeño hot sauce

When your veloute is thick, add the cheese. Stir until melted, then slowly add the cream. Remove from the heat when you have a thick sauce and add your seasonings. Keep warm.

Sauce Veloute

Sauce veloute is a base sauce designed to be piggy-backed by fancier fish-flavoured sauces such as lobster or oyster sauce. All you would do is add the requisite chopped ingredients to your veloute.

2 tbl butter
2 tbl flour

1 cup (8 fl oz/250 ml) fish stock
salt and pepper to taste

Melt the butter. Add the flour and cook until golden. Add the stock and cook until the required thickness is reached – `about 2 minutes. Remove from heat and add seasoning.

Softshell Crab Sandwich

Blue crabs start shedding their hard shells with the first full moon of May, or so they say at the southernmost tip of Maryland, known locally as the Eastern Shore. It is the softshell crab capital of the world, and fried softshell crabs are a sweet and crunchy delight. There is no substitute.

For the batter
1 cup (8 fl oz/250 ml) buttermilk
5 chives, snipped and finely chopped
2 eggs, beaten

For the flour mix
1/2 cup (2 1/2 oz/60 g) all-purpose flour
1 tsp cayenne
1/2 tsp paprika
1/2 tsp garlic salt
1/2 tsp garlic powder

6 softshell crabs – 'hotels' (4-inch shell span)
are my preferred size
peanut oil for shallow frying

To dress the crabs
6 burger buns, toasted
mayonnaise to spread
tomato slices for each bun
enough oak leaf lettuce leaves to cover each bun
jalapeno hot sauce to season
Old Bay Seasoning for a final sprinkle

First mix the batter. Then sift the ingredients for the flour mix together. Dip each crab in the batter, then in the flour mix. Heat a skillet to a moderate temperature. Shallow-fry the crabs in the oil. Do not crowd and turn once. They take about 5 minutes to cook. Remove from the oil and drain on kitchen paper. Keep warm. Assemble the sandwich with the hot crab in the middle. Sprinkle with the seasoning and eat quickly. Serve with onion rings (see below).

Onion Rings

These plain and simple onion rings make the perfect side order to just about any sandwich you care to mention.

1 large Spanish onion
1 cup (5 oz/125 g) all-purpose flour
1/2 tsp baking powder
1/4 tsp garlic salt

1 large egg, beaten
2/3 cup (7 fl oz/200 ml) beer
peanut oil to shallow-fry

Slice the onion and separate the rings. Whisk together all the other ingredients. Chill for a few hours. Heat about 2 inches of peanut oil to 375°F/190°C. Dip the onion rings in the batter and fry, without crowding, until golden brown. Drain on paper towels. Sprinkle with either sea salt or Kenny's French Quarter Seasoning (see p. 22). Serve immediately.

SIDE ORDERS AND OTHER STUFF

SIDE ORDERS and OTHER STUFF

Roast Garlic Bread Pudding

I first witnessed the idea of serving a bread pudding with an entree at Birks in the South Bay area of San Francisco, where I sampled a smoked prime rib with onion bread pudding and creamed spinach. I prefer to use garlic.

Eighty million pounds of garlic are produced annually in the US. About one third is processed by the Christopher Ranch in Gilroy, California – the garlic capital. During their peak season, beginning in July, a crew of 1,500 packs 150,000 pounds a day, for two months!

Simply soak 4 cups (5 slices) of white bread in milk, garlic puree, garlic salt and a little sugar for 5 hours. Mix in some beaten eggs and vanilla extract. Pre-heat your oven to 325°F/170°C/gas mark 3. Butter a casserole dish, pour in the bread mixture and bake for 1 hour or so. Your garlic pudding is ready when the top is browned and a toothpick comes out clean.

Blue Crab Claws

So called 'lump' meat is the white meat from the body of the crab. Claw meat is brownish and less well thought of. It is often used in recipes where appearance is not important. Yet for me it's the best part of the crab. A view shared by Joe's Stone Crab restaurant on Biscayne Street, Miami where crab claws are an institution. They sell crabs only between October and May. However, their Key Lime Pie is available, along with hash browns, all year long and they are both exceptional.

Serve as cocktail food with a wide range of dips and encourage folk to overindulge. Steaming the claws is easy. Dust the claws in Kenny's Seafood Seasoning (see p. 22) and place in a colander over a pot of boiling water. Place a cloth over the colander and steam until the claws are pink. Maybe serve the crabs with other steamed seafood such as crawfish, shrimp, oysters and clams. Get cracking.

These are my favorite dips for crab claws:

Aioli – add garlic and lemon to your home-made mayonnaise

Russian Dressing – add horseradish, cooked beets, onion, Worcestershire sauce and caviar to mayonnaise

Salsa Mayonnaise – add cored tomatoes, garlic, red onion, minced jalapenos and cilantro to mayonnaise

Boudin Sausage

Be careful, driver eating boudin', is a common bumper sticker in the south. Particularly in south Loiusiana. The steaming process, which is involved in their cooking, renders the casing a little tough. Consequently the idea is to bite into the sausage and pull out the contents. Hot boudin is a spicy mix of rice, cooked pork and onions. Garlic, sage, thyme, cayenne, allspice, mace and parsley make up the rest.

Conch Fritters with Key Lime Mustard Sauce

Conch to you probably means the classic spiral-shaped shell found on tropical shorelines. But to the folk of Florida it means the tasty little critter inside. Travelling through Florida, it is nigh on impossible to avoid the many restaurants selling conch, pronounced 'konk'. So popular is it down in southern Florida that folk from Key West are referred to as conchs. It can be served up in a variety of ways: I once ate a conch lasagne, cooked by the incomparable Norman Van Akens in Miami and had a glorious conch chowder at Bernard's Restaurant in Boynton Beach on Florida's Atlantic coast.

However, conch dipped in batter and deep-fried is the traditional way to serve the mollusc. Of all the joints where I have sampled these fritters, a little street stall outside Key West's tiny aquarium was the best. They are fried right in front of you and served with paper ramekins of tartar sauce and a chili sauce. The only hard part about cooking conch is the time spent in properly tenderizing the damn things – beat them with a mallet under a damp towel. If you cannot find conch – it will probably be frozen – substitute whelks. As an accompaniment I prefer my own Key Lime Mustard Sauce (see below).

3 cups (1 lb/450 g) conch meat
1 egg, beaten
¹/₃ cup (3 fl oz/75 ml) milk
1 cup (5 oz/125 g) all-purpose flour
2 tsp baking powder
¹/₂ tsp salt

¹/₂ tsp celery seeds
1 tbl white onion, minced
¹/₂ tsp Kenny's Hot Sauce (see p. 26)
peanut oil for deep-frying, heated to 375°F/190°C

Put the conch through a food grinder or pound with a mallet and chop into tiny pieces. Mix with all the other ingredients except the oil. With two teaspoons, form the batter into balls and drop in the oil. Fry until crispy. Drain on paper towels.

Key Lime Mustard Sauce

1 cup (8 fl oz/250 ml) mayonnaise
1 tbl Dijon mustard
1 tbl lime juice
1 tsp lime zest
1 tsp Kenny's Hot Sauce (see p. 26)
1/2 tsp Worcestershire sauce

1 tbl onion juice – grate 1 onion and keep the juice
1/2 tsp soy sauce
1/2 tsp oyster sauce
1 tsp Kenny's Seafood Seasoning (see p. 21)

Whisk all the ingredients together and chill for 2 hours. It tastes mighty fine.

Moors and Christians

This is black beans with white rice. Don't wait until tomorrow – it never comes, even if I feel it often belongs to me – just go to Key West, Florida, and sample the best black beans to be found anywhere. Pepe's on Caroline Street is the oldest eating house in the Florida Keys. It was established in 1909. Black beans and rice is not actually on their menu, but order the black bean soup with a side order of rice – it'll kill you and make you want to shout 'ashen lady give up your vows!'.

Cook your beans as normal, but add some aromatic vegetables braised in salt pork or country ham. I use ground cumin as the pronounced seasoning.

Flying Fish

This stew is the typical way of cooking flying fish in Barbados, where it is considered a delicacy.

2 tbl Kenny's Seafood Seasoning (see p. 21)
2 tbl all-purpose flour
juice of 1 lime
8 flying fish – 2 per person

For the sauce
2 tbl unsalted butter
1 red, 1 green and 1 yellow bell pepper (all medium size), topped, tailed and cored

(keep the ends for another use); cut off the veins then thinly slice the peppers
5 plum tomatoes, roasted, peeled, cored, then cut into small strips
1 red onion, sliced
1/2 cup (4 fl oz/125 ml) white wine
1 tsp oregano
1/2 tsp coarse-ground black pepper

Mix the seasoning and flour. Brush the lime over the fish then dredge them in the flour. Place under the broiler, set at a moderate heat, and cook for 5 minutes on both sides. At the same time, melt the butter and saute your vegetables. Once the onion is soft, add the wine and seasoning. Cook over a high heat until the sauce is nearly thick. Spoon a little of the sauce over the grilled fish and serve.

When serving fish on the bone, you always need to have bread or potatoes on the table. This is in case a bone gets stuck in one of your guest's throat. They quickly drag the offender down.

Corn Dogs

Has anyone ever muttered to you, with a full mouth, 'I'm crazy about you, baby'? Well this is what came out of my mouth when I first ate these at the Mobil gas station on Roosevelt and Duval in Key West. Fried sauasage in cornbread served on a stick was created in 1942 by Texan Neil Fletcher. It was originally called Fletcher's Original State Fair Corny Dog, but this was an even bigger mouthful than the dog itself.

For the sausage
1 ¹/₂ cups (8 oz/185 g) mashed chorizo
1 small white onion, finely diced
1 tsp cayenne
1 tsp garlic salt
2 tbl chicken stock

For the cornmeal batter
1 cup (5 oz/125 g) cornmeal

1 cup (5 oz/125 g) all-purpose flour
3 tsp baking powder
¹/₄ tsp sea salt
1 tbl sugar
2 tbl unsalted butter, melted
2 eggs, beaten
³/₄ cup (6 fl oz/175 ml) full-fat milk

Fry the sausage ingredients together for 10 minutes and drain. Mix well.

To make the cornmeal batter, first sift the dry ingredients together. Then gently mix in the butter, eggs and milk.

Then comes the tricky bit. If you have corn stick pans you're on a winner. But I'll assume you don't, just like your streets aren't paved with love. On a stretch of 6 x 4-inch cling film, spread 3 oz/70 g of the cormeal mix. Half fill it with the sausage mix. Cover with more cornmeal mix. Wrap in the cling film and roll tight – you want a cigar shape. Repeat until all the product is used up, then refrigerate for 1 hour. Insert an 8-inch wooden skewer half-way up the dog.

The next bit is up to you. I prefer to fry the corn dogs in peanut oil until the casing is crusty, but you can bake them, or do whatever you want with them. It's really is up to you.

Practise first and then make too many – they are so moreish. Of course you have to serve them with mustard, ketchup and hot sauce. Forget all the traditional pickled rubbish.

A-1 Sauce

This is the original steak sauce. It has been around since the mid-1800s and today it is owned by Nabisco. And this is my attempt at replicating the great product using the ingredients listed on the bottle. I have omitted the caramel coloring and the xantham gum, simply because I couldn't find them in my local store. Vegetable gums are added to bottled products, like hot sauces, to improve their viscosity. Instead I have added a few of my own favorites.

2 cups (16 fl oz/500 ml) water
1/2 cup (4 fl oz/125 ml) tomato puree
1/2 cup (4 fl oz/ 125 ml) distilled vinegar
1 tbl corn syrup
1 tbl raisin paste – you will probably have to make your own; get out your pestle and mortar
1 tsp garlic salt

1 tbl Curry Seasoning (see p. 24)
1 tbl mixed herbs
1/2 cup (4 fl oz/125 ml) orange juice
1 tbl lemon juice
1 tbl grapefruit juice
1 tbl orange zest
1 tbl dried garlic
1 tbl dried onion

Combine all ingredients in a thick-bottomed pot. Simmer for an hour or until thick. Allow to cool, then transfer to a Mason jar and seal. Store in a dark place for a week before using.

You may want to double or treble the recipe, as it will be used up pretty fast.

Guava Barbecue Sauce

This is an alternative, albeit complicated sauce, which is suitable for any strong-flavored fish such as salmon or tuna. Guava is an egg-shaped fruit, with a flavor that hints at honey, melon and strawberries. Due to its annoying seeds it's best to buy it in paste or nectar form.

1 red onion, finely diced

2 tbl unsalted butter

2 red bell peppers, smoked, peeled, cored and diced

2 white onions, smoked, and finely diced

6 tomatoes, smoked, peeled, cored and diced

2 cups (16 fl oz/500 ml) chicken stock

1/2 cup (4 fl oz/125 ml) ketchup

1 tsp Worcestershire sauce

1 tsp A-1 Sauce (see above)

1 tsp soy sauce

1 tsp oyster sauce

1 tbl cider vinegar

2 tbl brown sugar

1 tbl chipotle en adobe

1 tbl black mustard seeds

2 tbl guava paste

In a saucepan, saute the red onion in the butter. Add the smoked vegetables (small smokers are readily available and real easy to use) and cook for a further 5 minutes.

Add the chicken stock and bring to a simmer. Add the rest of the ingredients and cook over a low heat for 1 hour, or until the sauce is thick. Allow to cool, then transfer to a Mason jar and seal. Store in a dark place. The sauce will be ready to use in a couple of days.

Pretzels

A pretzel, as I'm sure you'll know, is a crisp salted type of biscuit, usually twisted into a loose knot. The first commercial pretzel bakery was set up in 1861 by Julius Sturgis and Ambrose Rauch in Litiz, Pennsylvania. My favorite commercial variety is the fat-free sourdough pretzels made by Snyders of Hanover, also in Pennsylvannia. Of course, I prefer to make my own at home using a bagel dough (see p. 47) flavored with onion.

Cut the dough into strips and roll into 6-inch rope-like lengths. Form each piece of dough into a horseshoe shape, the bottom of the shoe facing you. Pull the ends together for an oblong shape. Take one end up to the middle of the oblong, and do the same with the other end, but to the other side – press into place.

Boil the pretzel as detailed in my bagel recipe. Place the finished product in a bowl of koshering salt and shake vigorously, then bake for 20 minutes in an oven, pre-heated to 425°F/220°C/gas mark 7. This should take them to a nice golden brown. Serve them whilst still warm.

JUST
DESSERTS

JUST DESSERTS

Dessert is something I can take or leave. I prefer to indulge in what are called, innocuously, 'after-dinner drinks'. Anyways, for those of you with a sweeter disposition than myself, here is a brief selection of some of the more interesting Stateside desserts.

Garnets in Blood

This a simple dessert, and one even I can cope with. It's served at Cafe Pasqual in Santa Fe.

4 pomegranates
1 cup (8 fl oz/250 ml) Rioja, or any
full-bodied red wine

granulated sugar

Let your guests perform the operation themselves. Peel the pomegranates. Empty the seeds and meat into serving bowls. Cover the seeds with wine and mix in sugar to personal taste. Eat as soon as the sugar has dissolved. This is a good dessert to serve after a hearty, spicy meal.

Marvels

These deep-fried pastries date back to 19th-century Charleston. They are similar to *les oreilles de cochon*, 'pigs ears', which you can find in north-west Louisiana.

2 ³/₄ cups (13 ³/₄ oz/340 g) all-purpose flour
²/₃ cup (4 oz/100 g) unsalted butter
1 tbl sugar

3 large eggs, beaten
lard for frying
icing sugar for garnish

Sift the flour into your mixing bowl. Evenly cut in the butter. Mix the sugar into the eggs. Blend the eggs into the flour but do not knead, we need the dough quite light. Cover the dough and refrigerate for an hour or so.

Roll out the dough on a floured surface. You want it quite thin. Cut into any shape you fancy. Heat the lard to 370°F/185°C and fry your marvels until golden brown. Drain on a wire rack. Serve dusted with the icing sugar.

Strawberry Sorbet with Rose Water

This dish is from Portland, Oregon, known as the Rose City, after its terraced rose garden which contains over 10,000 rose bushes – a sensational sight when in bloom.

1 ³/₄ cups (14 fl oz/425 ml) water
2 cups (10 oz/250 g) sugar

3 cups (1 lb/450 g) strawberries
2 tsp rose water

Heat the water and sugar together in a saucepan until the sugar dissolves. Puree the strawberries. If the blender has trouble, add a little of the sugar to help. Blend together the strawberries, the sugar syrup and rose water. Freeze in your ice cream machine or just freeze in small batches. If you choose the latter, you will need to remove from the freezer once or twice and beat again to break up the ice crystals.

To make your own rose water, gather a ¹/₂ cup (2 ¹/₂ oz/60 g) rose petals. Place them in a shallow bowl and bruise the petals. Cover with 2 cups (16 fl oz/500 ml) water. Let the water stand for 2 hours. Strain and store in a sealed container or bottle.

Gooseberry Jelly

Alice B. Toklas was a marvellous cook. Her anecdotal tales of Gertrude Stein, Picasso and Matisse are as piquant as her writing is informative. She recalls in her *Cookbook* a spit-roasted lamb, basted with fresh mint and served with iced souffle and gooseberry jelly. The gooseberry jelly works with dark meats, just in the same way as redcurrants and cranberries. But I like to serve the jelly with baked fruit pies.

Simmer 9 cups (3lb/1.2 kg) gooseberries in 5 cups (2 pints/1.25 litres) water. Cook until the berries are tender. Strain the juice, pressing the flesh hard. Weigh the juice. Then boil for 10 minutes. Add an equal weight of sugar and bring to the boil again. Cook for 15 minutes or until you have a jelly.

Margarita Pie

The famous Key Lime Pie has its home in Key West, Florida. And the finest exponent is probably The Pier House restaurant. I adapted the accepted recipe to include tequila and cointreau, and consequently rename it Margarita Pie.

For a 9-inch biscuit crust
1 ½ cups (7 ½ oz/185 g) cookie crumbs, crushed
6 tbl melted butter
¼ cup(1 ¼ oz/30 g) granulated sugar

4 eggs, separated
1 14 oz/350 g can condensed milk
½ cup (4 fl oz/125 ml) lime juice
½ tsp baking powder
1 tbl gold tequila
1 tbl Cointreau

Use digestives to make your biscuit crust. In the States the Graham cracker would be first choice. Crush the biscuits and mix with the melted butter until they hold together. Form over the bottom of your baking tin, spring-form is best, and bake for 5 minutes on a high heat. Let cool.

Pre-heat the oven to 325°F/170°C/gas mark 3. In your blender mix the egg yolks until thick. Turn off the power and add the condensed milk. Pulse a few times. Add half the lime juice and the baking powder. Pulse a few times again, then add the rest of the lime juice and the liquors. Pulse once. Gently pour the mix into the pie crust. Bake in a bain marie – a dish half filled with water – for 20 minutes. Turn the oven off and open the door. Allow to cool in the oven for 30 minutes.

Traditionally the pie should be topped with meringue (hence the separated eggs), and then frozen. I like neither idea, but it's up to you. Garnish with lime zest and maybe serve with pouring cream.

My Perfect Pie Crust

This makes a great base for almost any pie filling you could mention including the couple of recipes below.

2 cups (10 oz/250 g) all-purpose flour
1/2 tsp salt

3/4 cup (3 3/4 oz/90 g) lard
5 tbl tepid water

Sift the flour and salt into a large mixing bowl. Cut in the lard and mix with your fingers until you have a cornmeal like texture. Sprinkle over the water and mix in, we want a moist dough. Form into a ball. Cover with cling film and chill for 40 minutes or until needed. This should be enough to line a 9-inch pie tin and top with a lid.

Apple Pie

What could be more American? Delicious.

8 medium cooking apples, peeled, cored and
stewed in water for 10 minutes
¹/₂ cup (2 ¹/₂ oz/60 g) brown sugar
1 tsp butter, melted

¹/₄ tsp ground cinnamon
pinch of ground cloves
1 tbl dark rum

Pre-heat the oven to 375°F/190°C/gas mark 5.

Mix the ingredients together and pour into the pie crust (see p. 199). Place the pastry lid over the filling, seal and trim the edges. Brush the top with an egg white and water glaze. Sprinkle over a little sugar.

Bake for 55 minutes or until golden brown.

Cherry Pie

What could be more American than apple pie? Try cherry pie. Although the cherry originated in Asia, the States is now the world's leading producer.

1 lb/2 cups fresh pitted cherries
¹/₂ cup (2 ¹/₂ oz/60 g) sugar
3 tbl cornstarch

3 tbl butter
1 tbl ground cinnamon
1 tsp ground nutmeg

Pre-heat the oven to 350°F/180°C/gas mark 4. Cook the cherries in a pan over a low flame for 5 minutes. (If you use fresh cherries, add 1 cup (8 fl oz/250 ml) water, otherwise they'll be too dry.) Allow to cool, then mix in the other ingredients. Return to a low flame and cook for 5 minutes. Pour into the unbaked pie shell (see p. 199). Top with more pastry and bake for 45 minutes. To serve your pie *à la mode*, charge 45 cents extra.

Next time you are heading to Chicago in July why not stop off on the 5th at Eau Claire for the Pit-Spit Festival held at the Tree-Mendus Fruit Farm. Now in its 24th year the contest is a 'global demonstration of how healthy eating, deep breathing and physical exercise can be accomoplished simultaneously, with only a minimal loss of dignity'. Traditionally, you try and spit a cherry stone as far as you can. The event is so much fun I even dreamt up a cherry pie recipe.

If you fancy something a little different, head to Lewistown, Montana. Here there is a Chokecherry Festival. The chokecherry – *prunus virginia* – is best served as jelly or a syrup because it's kinda bitter tasting. Chokecherries look like small clusters of grapes.

My Definitive New York Cheesecake

I tasted somebody else's New York cheesecake many years ago at a restaurant called Serendipity at 225 East 60th Street. It was quite a revelation: a complex cheesy dessert with a cake-like texture. Nothing like the packaged garbage you buy in supermarkets. It really is worth making your own New York-style cheesecake from scratch.

Serendipity also produces a fudge pie which, according to legend, was a big favorite with Marilyn Monroe. What follows is the basic New York cheesecake. You may wish to play with additional flavors. Various fruit zests work well.

For the base
1 ½ cups (8 oz/185 g) cookie crumbs, crushed
6 tbl melted butter
¼ cup (1 ¼ oz/30 g) granulated sugar

6 cups (2 lb/300 g) cream cheese
¾ cup (3 ¾ oz/90 g) granulated sugar
2 large eggs, lightly beaten
1 tsp vanilla extract
1 tbl baking powder
1 cup (8 fl oz/250 ml) sour cream

Pre-heat the oven to 350°F/180°C/gas mark 4. Mix the base ingredients together and form evenly over the bottom of a 9-inch spring-form pan. Chill the crust for 10 minutes. Bake for 10 minutes and allow to cool.

Beat the cream cheese and sugar together until smooth. Beat in the eggs, vanilla and baking powder. Stir in the sour cream until the mixture is well blended. Pour the mixture into the prepared crust and bake for 30 to 40 minutes. Turn the heat off, open the door and allow the cake to cool in the oven for 2 hours.

Maple-Pecan and Sweet Potato Pie

This recipe uses three of the most traditional American ingredients. Pecan pie is common in many restaurants today. Adding sweet potato is a quirky Louisiana twist.

1 9-inch pie crust (see p. 201)

Meringue mix
3 large eggs, plus 1 egg yolk
1/2 cup (2 1/2 oz/60 g) brown sugar
2 tbl unsalted butter, melted
1 tsp vanilla essence
4-5 tbl maple syrup
1 1/2 cups (8 oz/185 g) pecans, coarsely chopped

Potato mix
2 1/2 cups (12 1/2 oz/310 g) sweet potatoes, peeled, cubed and cooked until fork tender, then cooled
1/4 tsp ground ginger
1/4 tsp ground cinnamon
pinch of cloves
2 egg whites
1/3 cup (2 oz/45 g) sugar

Pre-heat oven to 350°F/180°C/gas mark 4. Combine eggs, egg yolk and brown sugar in a bowl. Stir until sugar has dissolved and the mixture is smooth. Blend in the butter, vanilla and maple syrup. Sprinkle pecans over the base of the pastry shell and top with the syrup mix.

Bake in the oven for 30 minutes max. Cool to room temperature.

Mix the sweet potatoes with the spices until smooth. In a large bowl beat the egg whites until frothy. Gradually add the sugar and continue beating until stiff peaks form. Fold the meringue into the sweet potato mix. Gently spoon the mixture over the pecans and syrup and smooth the surface. Bake in the oven for 20 minutes or until the filling has set.

Black and Blueberry Cobbler

This is a fruit dessert with a thick crust. There is no definitive recipe or even name — in New England it is called Bird's Nest Pudding. In Connecticut it is served with custard, but no topping. In Massachusetts maple syrup is de rigeur, whereas in Vermont a sour sauce is the accompaniment. I haven't included instructions for a crust as again there is no definitive recipe. Just use your own favorite.

1 pint blackberries, mash half
1 pint blueberries, mash half
1/2 cup (2 1/2 oz/60 g) sugar
1/4 tsp ground ginger

1/2 tsp ground cinnamon
pinch of allspice
2 tbl all-purpose flour
4 tbl unsalted butter

Pre-heat oven to 350°F/180°C/gas mark 4. In a casserole dish combine the fruit with the sugar, spices and flour. Dot with the butter. Bake for 25 minutes. Remove from oven.

THE LAST WORD

THE LAST WORD

I hope you enjoyed my tour of American cooking. There is so much more I wanted to tell you. Maybe we can meet again over another volume. I still need to tell you about Frogmore Stews, Minnehana, Beef-on-Weck ...

The food in America today is incredibly inspiring. The new wave of chefs is challenging the foundations of American cooking taking old traditions down new paths and leading America out of the gastronomic wilderness. I hope I've shown you some of these new twists on old ways and that this will encourage you to experiment and take risks in the kitchen yourself. We should all enjoy upsetting conventions. Above all, this is why I love cooking: just like falling in love – cook without a care.

Give me a call. e-mail <Kennycooks3@compuserve.com>

LAGNIAPPE

LAGNIAPPE

Place a tea towel or damp kitchen paper under your chopping board to stop it slipping.

Be careful when slicing bagels. According to Mark Smith, head of George Washington Hospital's Department of Emergency Medicine, in Washington DC, the bagel is one of the greatest safety hazards in the American home.

I presume you always buy fresh Parmesan. I now suggest you save the rind for your soups. It enlivens soups like you just don't know — especially minestrone.

Ninety per cent of the States' artichokes come from Monterey County in California — I knew I had a serious reason for not visiting the place.

Folk in the States say to soak onions in water before chopping if you want to avoid the tears. Baloney! Just learn to chop faster. Why let the water have your flavors?

The McDonald's in Lake Tahoe City has no golden arches, but does boast a glassed-in woodburning fireplace. Who cares? They still help to corrupt millions of folk into believing food comes in a styrofoam box and, similarly, that it is cool to eat in the street. The original native Americans ate better by far.

Vine-ripened tomatoes doesn't mean a tomato that has been left on the vine to ripen. It means a green tomato with a slightly pink blush, left to ripen on the counter. Never refrigerate them — unless you hate the tomato flavor.

As well as being a shield against werewolves and vampires, garlic contains an antiseptic oil. In its raw state it can be used as a poultice, for treating high and low blood pressure and also nervous disorders. Apparently it thins the blood and simultaneously raises body heat, thus it is considered an aphrodisiac — providing both of you eat it, heh?

To keep limes properly, sprinkle them with water and place them in a plastic bag. Close the bag and refrigerate.

In Oregon a hazlenut is called a filbert. In 2830 BC the filbert was listed as one of the five sacred nourishments in China.

Turkeys don't stand in the rain, head up, beak open, as a suicide ritual. They do it as a natural instinct to stop themselves becoming wet and cold. The rain runs off their feathers. Now you know!

The Los Angeles Dodgers, who play at the 56,000-capacity Dodger Stadium, annually sell 659,000 bags of peanuts.

The Bay Wolf restaurant in Oakland always offers duck on the menu — I'll never go.

Panko is white Japanese breadcrumbs.

Never stand up in a canoe.

BIBLIOGRAPHY

Bibliography

LOUISIANA REAL & RUSTIC, Emeril Lagasse, William Morrow, 1996

THE AMERICAN KITCHEN, Ellen M. Plante, Facts on File, 1995

LA PARILLA, Reed Hearon, Chronicle, 1996

FLAVORED BREADS, Mark Miller, Ten Speed Press, 1996

THE SAN FRANCISCO CHRONICLE COOKBOOK, eds Micheal Bauer and Frank Irwin, 1997

THE COMPLETE BOOK OF SOUPS AND STEWS, Bernard Clayton, Jr, Fireside, 1984

KENNY'S CAJUN CREOLE COOKBOOK, Kenny Miller, Prion, 1996

THE MASTER & THE MARGARITA, Mikhail Bulgakov, Grove Press, 1967

CHARCUTERIE, Jane Grigson, Michael Joseph, 1967

THE ART OF EATING, M.F.K. Fisher, Vintage, 1976

FOOD FROM AN AMERICAN FARM, Janeen Aletta Sarlin, Simon & Schuster, 1991

TROUT FISHING IN AMERICA, Richard Brautigan, Jonathan Cape, 1970

JOY OF COOKING, Rombauer & Becker, Dent, 1931

AMERICAN CHARCUTERIE, Victoria Wise, Penguin, 1987

BISCUITS, SPOONBREAD, AND SWEET POTATO PIE, Bill Neal, 1990

DUNGENESS CRABS AND BLACKBERRY COBBLER, Janie Hibler, Knopf, 1996

I HEAR AMERICA COOKING, Betty Fussel, Viking Penguin, 1986

INDEX

A-1 sauce 192
acorn squash soup with smoked chicken 74-5
aioli 187
anadama bread 157
ancho-olive oil rub 37
appetizers 85-95
    chicken and papaya quesadilla with green
        chile chutney 86-7
    crab empanaditas with rocket salad and
        mustard oil 91-3
    eggplant pirogues with seafood gumbo gravy
        88-9
    flour tortilla 85-6
    mushroom quesadilla with corn salsa 91
    oyster Rockefeller 88-9
    rock shrimp hash 93-4
    shrimp patties with chipotle- herbsaint butter
        89-90
    turkey picadillo with hot tomato rum down
        sauce 94-5
apple
    and bacon chutney 107
    pie 200
avocado: guacamole 150

bagels 47
baked beans, Boston 175
banana cream pie 160-1
barbecue marinade 36
barbecue pork sandwich 177-8
barbecuing 123-4
beans
    black and white bean soup 79-80
    Boston baked 175
    Choctaw leather britches bean stew 135-6
    Moors and Christians 189-90
    navy bean and collared green soup 73
    re-fried pinto 134
beef
    Blackfoot gut with mushroom gravy 132-3
    burgers 162
    chile stew 78
    chili 150

meatball 'hero boy' 173
    philly cheesesteak 175-6
    sloppy Joe 170
    Stumptown stew 110-11
beer-braised onions 165
biscuits 51-2
    cheddar-jalapeño 115
black beans: Moors and Christians 189-90
black and blueberry cobbler 203-4
black and white bean soup 79-80
blackened chicken salad with molasses-
        buttermilk dressing 112-13
blackened red drum with toasted pecan butter
        and peach-tasso chutney 100-1
blackening seasoning 22
blackeyed pea salsa 128
Blackfoot gut with mushroom gravy 132-3
Bloody Mary 83-4
blue cheese-thousand island dressing 41
blue crab claws 186-7
blue fish, grilled, with island sherry sauce
        104-5
blueberry muffins 53-4
Boston baked beans 175
boudin sausage 187
bread
    burger bun 163-4
    spoonbread 140
    types of 156-7
    white loaf 55-6
bread pudding, garlic 186
Brunch 44-60
    bagels 47
    blueberry muffins 53-4
    eggs Benedict 52-3
    eggs and wet belly hash 49
    green chile cornbread 54
    grits with ham, red-eye gravy, eggs and
        biscuits 50-2
    ham and eggs Alexandria 60
    hash browns with rumbled eggs 59
    huevos rancheros 56-8
    pancakes 48

waffles 45
The Western 46
buffalo pot pie 129-30
burger bun 163-4
burgers 161-4
    accompanying sauces 165-6
    smoked chicken 163
butter
    chipotle-herbsaint 90
    garlic 41-2
    toasted pecan 100-1

cactus
    and pear salad 152
    salsa borracha 17-18
Caesar salad 144
callaloo: pepperpot stew 67
candied yams 138-9
Carolina perlow 68
catfish tacos with tequila creamed corn 98-9
cheddar-jalapeño biscuits 115
cheese
    Cuban cheese sandwich 168
    macaroni and 174
    Monte Cristo 180
    potato chips with maytag blue 103
    Santa Fe grilled cheese sandwich 167
cheesecake, New York 201-2
cheesesteak, philly 175-6
chef salad 146-7
cherry pie 200-1
chicken
    acorn squash soup with smoked 74-5
    blackened chicken salad with molasses-
        buttermilk dressing 112-13
    burger 163
    cacciatore 109-10
    fried 118-19
    fried chicken with mango-habañero chutney
        and spiced pumpkin muffins 125-7
    fried chicken salad 153-4
    hot browns 181
    marbella 105-6

    and papaya quesadilla with green chile
        chutney 86-7
    tortilla soup 71
chilaquiles 128-9
chile
    mustard 28
    pickled chile peppers 12-13
    stew 78
    varieties of 13
    verde 103
    see also individual types of chile
chili
    cheap 150
    seasoning 25
chipotle
    and herbsaint butter 90
    mayonnaise 179-80
    tomato soup with chipotle creme fraiche 75-6
chips 180-1
chive-jalapeño oil 34, 102
Choctaw leather britches bean stew 135-6
chowder
    creamed corn, with green chile salsa 76-7
    Long Island clam 70
    New England clam 69
chutney 30-2
    apple-bacon 107
    green chile 87
    mango, papaya and green chile 32
    mango-habañero 126
    peach-habañero 31
    peach-tasso 101
cioppino 66
clams
    Long Island clam chowder 70
    New England clam chowder 69
Cobb salad 145
cocktails *see* drinks
coleslaw 138
conch fritters with key lime mustard
    sauce 188-9
Coney Island red hots 170
corn

creamed 137-8
creamed corn chowder with green chile salsa
    76-7
dogs 191-2
guidelines for choosing 19
ham succotash with cheddar-jalapeño biscuits
    113-15
salsa 18-19
salsa with mushroom quesadilla 91
tequila creamed 99
cornbread
    crackling 64
    green chile 54
    spinach 122-3
corned beef: eggs and wet belly hash 49
crab
    claws 186-7
    empanaditas with rocket salad and mustard oil
        91-3
    louls 147-8
    sandwich 182-3
    soup 65
crackling cornbread 64
crawfish, sauteed 117
creamed corn 137-8
creamed corn chowder with green chile salsa
    76-7
Cuban cheese sandwich 168
curry seasoning 24

debris po'boy 168
desserts 196-204
    apple pie 200
    banana cream pie 160-1
    black and blueberry cobbler 203-4
    cherry pie 200-1
    garnets in blood 196
    gooseberry jelly 198
    maple-pecan and sweet potato pie 202-3
    Margarita pie 198-9
    marvels 196-7
    New York cheesecake 201-2

strawberry sorbet with rose water 197
dips 187
dressing(s) 37-41
    blue cheese-thousand island 41
    honey-mustard 39
    Kenny's ranch 38
    molasses-buttermilk 113
    Russian 187
    tomato French 40
    tuna 147
    vinaigrettes 32-3
drinks 82-4
    Bloody Mary 83-4
    Manhattan 83
    Margarita 82-3
    Martini 84

eggplant pirogues with seafood gumbo gravy 88-9
eggs
    Benedict 52-3
    ham and eggs Alexandria 60
    hash browns with rumbled 59
    huevos rancheros 56-8
    and wet belly hash 49
empanaditas, crab, with rocket salad and
        mustard oil 91-3

fiesta salad 148-50
fish
    cioppino 66
    flying 190
    gefilte 136-7
    Gulf Coast gumbo 62-3
    see also individual names; seafood
flour tortilla 85-6
flying fish 190
French fries 162
French quarter seasoning 21-2
fried chicken 118-19
fried chicken salad 153-4
frits with ham, red-eye gravy, eggs and biscuits
    50-2
fruit salsa 16-17

garlic
  bread pudding 186
  butter 41-2
  mustard 29
garnets in blood 196
gefilte fish 136-7
gooseberry jelly 198
gravy
  mushroom 133
  white 122
Greek salad 103
green beans: Choctaw leather britches bean stew 135-6
green chile
  burger sauce 165-6
  chutney 87
  cornbread 54
  salsa 77
  sauce 58
greens
  pot likker 121
  turnip or mustard 120-1
guacamole 150
guava barbecue sauce 193
guinea fowl with re-fried pinto beans and zuni succotash 133-4
gumbo, Gulf coast 62-3

ham
  and eggs Alexandria 60
  succotash with cheddar-jalapeño bisquits 113-15
hash
  eggs and wet belly 49
  rock shrimp 93-4
hash browns with rumbled eggs 59
Hollandaise sauce 52
honey-mustard dressing 39
hot browns 181
hot dog 170
hot sauces 25-6
huevos rancheros 56-8

island sherry sauce 104-5

jalapeño
  cheddar-jalapeño biscuits 115
  and chive oil 34, 102
  cream of jalapeño soup 71-2
jambalaya cakes with sauteed crawfish and old-fashioned tomato sauce 116-17
jelly, gooseberry 198
jerked fried chicken with mango-habañero chutney and spiced pumpkin muffins 125-7

Kenny's ranch dressing 38
ketchup 27
  mushroom 164-5
key lime mustard sauce 189

lime
  mustard 29
  mustard sauce 189
lobster
  club sandwich 179-80
  Newburg 141-2
Long Island clam chowder 70

Macadamia-crusted mahi-mahi with tamarind sauce and tomato-tartar sauce 108-9
macaroni and cheese 174
mahi-mahi, Macadamia-crusted, with tamarind sauce and tomato-tartar sauce 108-9
mango
  and habañero chutney 126
  papaya and green chile chutney 32
Manhattan, The 83
maple-pecan and sweet potato pie 202-3
Margarita 82-3
Margarita pie 198-9
marinade 34-6
  barbecue 36
  tequila and cilantro 35
  tomato and bourbon 35
Martini 84
marvels 196-7
mashed potatoes 120
mayonnaise 30, 148

chipotle 179-80
remoulade sauce 38-9
salsa 187
meatball 'hero boy' 173
medicine sausage 134-5
molasses-buttermilk dressing 113
Monte Cristo 180
Moors and Christians 189-90
mornay sauce 181
muffins
blueberry 53-4
spiced pumpkin 126-7
muffuletta 176
mushroom
gravy 133
ketchup 164-5
quesadilla with corn salsa 91
mustard 28-9
chile 28
garlic 29
and honey dressing 39
lime 29
lime mustard sauce 189
oil 93
onion 29
mustard greens 120-1

navy bean and collared green soup 73
New England clam chowder 69
New York cheesecake 201-2

oil 33-4
chive-jalapeño 34
jalapeño-chive 102
mustard 94
omelette 46
onion(s)
beer-braised 165
mustard 29
rings 183
oyster(s)
Rockefeller 88-9

tautog with curried oysters and apple-bacon
chutney 106-7

pancakes 48
papaya
chicken and papaya quesadilla with green
chile chutney 86-7
mango, papaya and green chile chutney 32
Parker House rolls 157
pastries 196-7
pastrami 169
patties, shrimp 89-90
Pawnee roast guinea fowl with re-fried pinto
beans and zuni succotash 133-4
peach
and habañero chutney 31
and tasso chutney 101
pecan
butter 100-1
crusted pan-fried trout with jalapeño-chive oil
101-2
maple-pecan and sweet potato pie 202-3
pepper(s)
pickled chile 12-13
red and black pepper rub 36-7
seasoning 24
pepperpot stew 67
perlow, Carolina 68
philly cheesesteak 175-6
picadillo, turkey, with hot tomato rum down
sauce 94-5
pickled chile peppers 12-13
pico de gallo 19
pie
apple 200
banana cream 160-1
buffalo pot 129-30
cherry 200-1
maple-pecan and sweet potato 202-3
Margarita 198-9
pie crust 199
pig's feet 139
pinto beans, re-fried 134

pizza 130-1
pomegranates: garnets in blood 196
pork: barbecue pork sandwich 177-8
pork chops, smothered 140-1
pot likker 121
pot pie, buffalo 129-30
potato(es)
    chips 180-1
    chips with maytag blue cheese 103
    French fires 162
    mashed 120
    salad 171
    slaw 178
pretzels 194
pumpkin muffins, spiced 126-7

rattlesnake salsa 16
razorback sopping sauce 178-9
red and black pepper rub 36-7
red chile sauce 73
red drum, blackened, with toasted pecan butter
    and peach-tasso chutney 100-1
red snapper ceviche salad with blackeyed pea
    salsa 127-8
remoulade sauce 38-9
rice
    Carolina perlow 68
    jambalaya cakes with sauteed crawfish and
        old-fashioned tomato sauce 116-17
    seafood dirty 118
roast corn salsa 18-19
roast garlic bread pudding 186
roast tomato soup with chipotle creme fraiche
    75-6
rock shrimp hash 93-4
rocket salad 92-3
rolls, Parker House 157
rubs 34
    ancho-olive oil 37
    red and black pepper 36-7
Rueben sandwich 169

Russian dressing 187
salad(s) 144-54
    blackened chicken, with molasses- buttermilk
        dressing 112-13
    cactus and pear 152
    Caesar 144
    chef 146-7
    Cobb 145
    crab louis 147-8
    fiesta 148-50
    fried chicken 153-4
    Greek 103
    potato 171
    red snapper ceviche, with blackeyed pea salsa
        127-8
    rocket 92-3
    tortilla 151
    see also dressings
Sally Lunn 156
salsa 14-20
    blackeyed pea 128
    borracha 17-18
    corn 18-19
    fresca 14-15
    green chile 77
    mayonnaise 187
    pico de gallo 19
    rattlesnake 16
    tropical fruit 16-17
    verde 15
    xnipec 20
sandwich(es) 156-73
    barbecue pork 177-8
    Cuban cheese 168
    debris po'boy 168
    hot browns 181
    lobster club 179-80
    meatball 'hero boy' 173
    Monte Cristo 180
    muffuletta 176
    philly cheesesteak 175-6
    Rueben 169

Sante Fe grilled cheese 167
sloppy Joe 170
softshell crab 182-3
Sante Fe grilled cheese sandwich 167
sauce(s)
   A-1 192
   chile verde 103
   green chile 58
   green chile burger 165-6
   guava barbecue 193
   Hollandaise 52
   hot 25-6
   island sherry 104-5
   lime mustard 189
   mornay 181
   razorback sopping 178-9
   red chile 73
   remoulade 38-9
   soy 39-40
   tamarind 108
   tomato 117
   tomato-tartar 108
   veloute 182
   white chili smothering 166
   see also chutneys; dressings; salsa
sausage
   Blackfoot gut with mushroom gravy 132-3
   boudin 187
   corn dogs 191-2
   medicine 134-5
saute seasoning 23
seafood
   dirty rice 118
   seasoning 21
   see also fish
seasoning 20-5
   blackening 22
   chili 25
   curry 24
   French quarter 21-2
   general 23
   pepper 24

saute 23
seafood 21
shrimp(s)
   Carolina perlow 68
   hash 93-4
   patties with chipotle-herbsaint butter 89-90
sloppy Joe 170-1
smoked chicken burger 163
smothered pork chops 140-1
softshell crab sandwich 182-3
sorbet, strawberry, with rose water 197
soup(s)
   acorn squash, with smoked chicken 74-5
   black and white bean 79-80
   crab 65
   cream of jalapeño 71-2
   navy bean and collared green 73
   roast tomato, with chipotle creme fraiche
      75-6
   tortilla 71
   see also chowder; stew(s)
soy sauce 39-40
spiced pumpkin muffins 126-7
spinach
   cornbread 122-3
   pepperpot stew 67
   wilted 90
spoonbread 140
squash soup with smoked chicken 74
steak *see* beef
stew(s)
   chile 78
   Choctaw leather britches bean 135-6
   cioppino 66
   Gulf Coast gumbo 62-3
   pepperpot 67
   Stumptown 110-11
   turkey picadillo with hot tomato rum down
      sauce 94-5
strawberry sorbet with rose water 197
Stumptown stew 110-11
succotash

ham, with cheddar-jalapeño bisquits 113-15
zuni 134

tamales 142-3
tamarind sauce 108
tautog with curried oysters and apple-
    bacon chutney 106-7
tequila
    and cilantro marinade 35
    creamed corn 99
tomatillos: Salsa Verde 15
tomato
    and bourbon marinade 35
    French dressing 40
    sauce 117
    soup with chipotle creme fraiche 75-6
    and tartar sauce 108
tortilla(s)
    catfish tacos with tequila creamed corn 98-9
    chicken and papaya quesadilla with green
        chile chutney 86-7
    chilaquiles 128-9
    flour 85-6
    mushroom quesadilla with corn salsa 91
    salad 151
    soup 71

tropical fruit salsa 16-17
trout: pecan-crusted pan-fried, with jalapeño-
    chive oil 101-2
tuna
    dressing 147
    melt 172
turkey picadillo with hot tomato rum down
    sauce 94-5
turnip greens 120-1

veloute sauce 182
vinaigrettes 32-3

waffles 45
walnut breakfast bread 157
Western, The 46
white bean soup 80
white chili smothering sauce 166
white gravy 122
white loaf 55-6

xnipec salsa 20

yams, candied 138-9

zucchini bread 157
zuni succotash 134